Single Malt & Scotch Whisky

Single Malt
&
Scotch
Whisky

Text & Photographs by
Daniel Lerner

KÖNEMANN

Published by
Black Dog & Leventhal Publishers Inc.
151 West 19th Street
New York, NY 10011

Front matter photography:
Robert M. Rothberg M.D. and
The Scotch Malt Whisky Society.

Book design and coordination:
Jonette Jakobson

Copyright © 1998 for this edition:
Könemann Verlagsgesellschaft mbH
Bonner Str. 126, D-50968 Köln

Production Manager: Detlev Schaper
Printing and binding by Kossuth Printing House Co.
Printed in Hungary
ISBN 3-8290- 0418-4

10 9 8 7 6 5 4 3 2

**Many thanks to the following people
whose help was invaluable:**

James Salzano
Dennis Milbauer
Cheryl To
Chris Cannon
Pamela Horn
Jonette Jakobson
J.P. Leventhal
Justin Lukach
Herb Lapchin, Park Avenue Liquor Shop, New York
Carolyn Schaffer
Robert M. Rothberg, M.D.
Alan Shayne
The Scotch Malt Whisky Society
Matt Gross, John Gross and Company Importers
Steve Meyers and Jeff Pogash, Schieffelin & Somerset
Joel McCabe, Heublein
Anne Riives, Bowmore
Ed Perez, Stock Distillerie
Dick Claftin, Remy Amerique
Marvin Shadman, Barton Brands
Jennifer Crowl, Seagrams
Bob Kopach, Jim Beam Brands
Dan Dabblet, White Rock Distributors
Pat Dwayne, European Beverage Company
Chris McCrory, Sazerac
Tom DeLuca, Austin Nichols
Michael Shaw, Paramount Brands
Caitlin Connelly, Kratz & Co.
George Acevedo, Peerless Distributors

Special thanks to
JUdson Grill
52 West 52nd Street
New York City

Contents

*The Glen running through
the Scottish Highlands*

Introduction

Imagine the Scottish Highlands around 500 A.D. A savagely beautiful landscape—rolling heather and peat-covered hills, pure water flowing from burns and springs, fields of ripe, golden barley gently swaying in the summer breeze. A group of Irish monks comes to visit. They bring with them a secret process, perhaps of their own invention, perhaps something they learned from visiting the Far East or India or Greece. "All this that is around you," says one of the monks, "we will turn into the water of life." (Or something to that effect.)

The procedure for producing a fermented, low-alcohol beverage was most likely already known by this time. But what a beverage! Unlike the beer of our day, the stuff that Highlanders drank 1,500 years ago must have resembled thin, alcoholic oatmeal. Then someone came along and turned this "beer" into light, pure, flavorful, highly alcoholic stuff. Water of life, indeed.

*T*he Distilling Process: No Ordinary

In Latin, the word "distill" means to trickle or drip down. Alcohol boils, conveniently, at a lower temperature than water. This simple rule is the basis for all distilling. Hot, boiled vapors are directed into tubes cooled by immersion in water. The result is condensation, in which the cooling vapors trickle back into a liquid state. But this description oversimplifies a time-honored, laborious process and the sublime product it yields. Making Scotch whisky is more like this:

Floor maltings are rarely seen nowadays, but at Benriach Distillery floor malters are still retained to turn the malt during germination to prevent matting.

Trickle

1. Pick some ripe barley.

2. Submerge it in local spring water for several days.

3. Spread the soaked grain out on a large flat surface—the floor of a barn will do nicely—and during the course of the next eight to ten days, turn it over each day with a large, flat, wooden shovel. Why? Because we want the barley to begin to germinate, to begin to sprout. Inside each grain, enzymes are converting starch to sugar. More later on how these sugars are converted to alcohol.

4. Take this wet, barely germinated barley and spread it out on the floor of a large kiln to malt. (When you visit a distillery in Scotland, look for the malting shed. It is the low building with the

The Benriach pagoda.

3

The malt kiln used for drying the sweet, malted barley.

The typical fuel used for drying malted barley is peat.

interesting pagoda-shaped ventilator on the roof.) Start a fire under the floor, fueling it with peat; it works well and there is lots of it close by. You are doing this to stop the barley from further germinating and—a nice bonus—peat, which is composed of highly compressed organic material, smokes when it burns. This smoke impregnates the grain and leaves a lovely smoky, peaty flavor in the finished product.

5. Clean the grain and grind it by passing it through a grist mill.

6. Place the grist in a large vat and add hot water. The local water often has trace minerals and some "peaty" quality, which imparts additional flavoring elements. The remaining starch in the grist is being converted into sugar, which is then dissolved into solution. Repeat this cycle of draining and adding hot water several times. You have now produced "wort," a sweet liquid.

Strathisla—the architecture lives on—but the distillery no longer functions.

*The Macallan Distillery
and barrel room*

The mill feed where the malted barley is ground before it is added to water.

7. Drain the liquid into a large, deep wooden vat and add brewer's yeast. Lots of action for the next two or three days: boiling, steaming and frothing. Fermentation is happening. (If you are a citizen of 500 A.D., you know how to do all this because so far it pretty much resembles the process by which you have been making beer.)

10

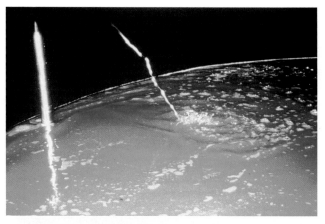

Malted barley is mixed with boiling water in the mash tun to create a syrup called wort.

After the wort has cooled, yeast is added and mixed in the wash back.

8. Now you are ready to implement the new (for the citizens noted above) technology: fill a heavy cauldron with the fermented liquid, which contains 5 to 9 percent alcohol and is now called "wash." Cover tightly. Place over a coal fire. Sticking out of the lid of the cauldron is a spout. Sprouting out of the spout is a coil of copper

Wooden wash backs are more classical of the whisky industry than steel wash backs.

tubing. This coil is generally submerged in a barrel of cold water (or some other arrangement, so long as cold water flows over the coils). As the vapors produced from the boiling of the wash rise through the spout and into the coils, the temperature changes inside. This causes the vapors, which contain oils, flavors, esters, alcohols, water and various other pure and not-so-pure agents, to condense and drip down the coils, to be collected in some sort of receptacle. After you have run all the wash through your still and collected it, clean the still, re-fire it, and repeat the process.

9. Having completed this first distillation, you now have in your possession a quantity of liquid known as the "low wines" (which contain 20 to 25 percent alcohol). To purify and concentrate the flavors and alcohol of this liquid, you embark upon a second distillation. From experience you know that at the beginning of this second distillation, the stuff that comes out first, called the "foreshots," is still pretty impure and not very drinkable, so you drain it off and save it to distill again with the next batch. Now, finally the "mid-

The Lowland–Glenkinchie Distillery.

dle cut," the stuff you have worked so hard to produce, is drawn off. After this is completed, all the "feints," that is, the remaining distillate, are drawn off and saved. This production is too impure and/or dilute to consume and will be mixed with the foreshots and the next batch of low wines for the next time you distill.

10. Mix a little gun powder (really!) with a little of your whisky and light the mixture. If it doesn't light, it's not strong enough; if it explodes, it's too

The Glen Grant Highland Distillery: Larger size stills suggest production of a lighter whisky.

Macallan maintains some of the smallest stills using direct heat for a more elegant, intense flavor.

strong. If it burns steadily, you have "proof."

11. Put the colorless whisky into casks. Sell most of your production to whisky merchants so you can pay the rent on the farm. These merchants will bottle it as they need it, selling right out of cask (no aging) for the average Joe and aged a bit in cask for the gentry (they can afford it). Of course, you keep a little for yourself to drink with your family and friends.

The dreaded gaugers used to maintain their excise posts next to the spirit safes. Now they are maintained by distillery workers.

Whether it's 1494, the date of the first recorded purchase of malted barley for the production of Aqua Vitae; or 1690, when Ferintosh, the first distillery mentioned by name, suffered a fire; or 1932, when America's Prohibition was repealed; or 1997, when Suntory, the Japanese beverage giant, acquired Macallan distillery—in 500 years, the process of distilling malt whisky has remained fundamentally unchanged.

SAMPLES   LOW WINES Nº 1.   WASH Nº 1.

Nº 1. SPIRIT & SAMPLES SAFE

Established 1786
Keith

No. 3 SAFE

Nº 3
WASH STILL

R G ABERCROMBIE & CO LTD

The Process

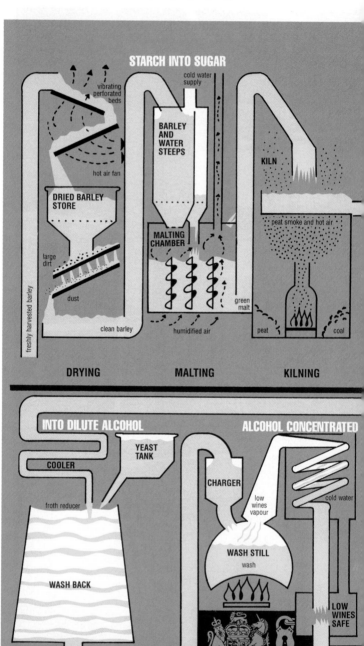

STARCH INTO SUGAR

cold water supply

vibrating perforated beds

BARLEY AND WATER STEEPS

hot air fan

KILN

DRIED BARLEY STORE

peat smoke and hot air

MALTING CHAMBER

large dirt

freshly harvested barley

dust

green malt

clean barley

humidified air

peat

coal

DRYING   **MALTING**   **KILNING**

INTO DILUTE ALCOHOL   **ALCOHOL CONCENTRATED**

YEAST TANK

COOLER

CHARGER

cold water

froth reducer

low wines vapour

WASH STILL

wash

LOW WINES SAFE

WASH BACK

DIEU ET MON DROIT

from this point on, production is under supervision of H.M. Customs & Excise

LOW WINES RECEIVER

FERMENTING   **DISTILLING**

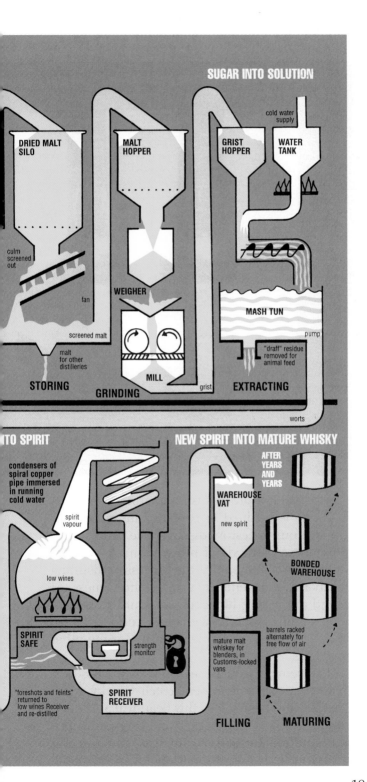

SUGAR INTO SOLUTION

DRIED MALT SILO

MALT HOPPER

GRIST HOPPER

WATER TANK

cold water supply

culm screened out

fan

WEIGHER

screened malt

malt for other distilleries

MILL

grist

MASH TUN

pump

"draff" residue removed for animal feed

STORING

GRINDING

EXTRACTING

worts

...TO SPIRIT

NEW SPIRIT INTO MATURE WHISKY

condensers of spiral copper pipe immersed in running cold water

spirit vapour

low wines

SPIRIT SAFE

strength monitor

"foreshots and feints" returned to low wines Receiver and re-distilled

SPIRIT RECEIVER

WAREHOUSE VAT

new spirit

AFTER YEARS AND YEARS

BONDED WAREHOUSE

barrels racked alternately for free flow of air

mature malt whiskey for blenders, in Customs-locked vans

FILLING

MATURING

*W*hy *Scotch Whisky?*

T he distilling process is fascinating, especially
if one is inclined to contemplate its origins.
How did our ancestors discover the process and
devise these methods of production? As a testa-
ment to human ingenuity, the process of distilling
is unrivaled in its efficiency and completeness. At
the end of the day, however, we could be talking
about distilling paint, gasohol, or rocket fuel, so
easily is the basic principle replicated using other
substances.

This being the case, we may now ask our-
selves where, exactly, does Scotch whisky come
from? From whence does this beautiful and poetic nectar, fully formed in each and every one of its
individual manifestations, emerge? The immedi-
ate answer to that question is obviously Scotland,

and more specifically, several regions within that country: the Highlands, the Lowlands, Islay, Campbeltown and Island. (Within these general regions are a series of sub-regions: the Highlands include the Northern Highlands, Speyside, the Eastern Highlands and Perthshire. Island encompasses Skye, Mull, Jura, and Orkney.)

Indeed, geography offers something of a clue to what makes this marvelous beverage, marvelous. But there are other essentials: the amount and quality of peat used in the malting process; the mineral content and flavor characteristics of the water used by the individual distillery; the distillery's proximity to the ocean; the type of barley; the degree of its germination and the intensity of malting; the style, shape, and general condition of the stills; the experience of the still master, and last but not least, the kind of barrel used for aging and maturing of the distillate. Nor should we forget fairies, wood, and water sprites, legendary historical figures and a host of other mythologies that populate Scotland and its whisky industry.

Macallan's official charting of the marrying casks.

Regional Magic

In a very broad sense, the whiskies from each of the regions have some identifiable characteristics.

The Highlands/Speyside: When the Scots refer to the Highlands, they're talking about the upper two-thirds of Scotland. Everything that one associates with Scotland in terms of customs, language, and even plaid, comes largely from this region.

The river Spey, which runs through the Highlands, has the greatest concentration of distilleries now in Scotland, hence the sub-region known as Speyside. The whiskies from this area tend to be sweet, clean, rather subtle, and layered with pronounced fruity and honeyed notes.

At the heart of whisky country in the Highlands is the river Spey. This water is famous for great whisky and great salmon fishing.

A trip to the Highlands is always magical, especially at the Glen Grant Distillery. A walk through the recently restored gardens is topped off by a dram of the distillery's finest. (The keys to this vault are held only by the Distillery Manager and possibly one other person).

The
Malt
Whisky
producing
regions
of Scotland

| Campbeltown |
| Highland/ Speyside |
| Islands |
| Islay |
| Lowland |

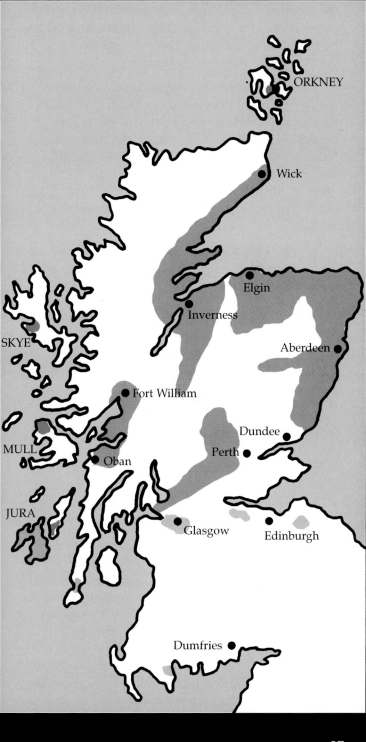

ORKNEY

Wick

Elgin

Inverness

SKYE

Aberdeen

Fort William

Dundee

MULL

Perth

Oban

JURA

Glasgow

Edinburgh

Dumfries

27

The desolate landscape and harsh climate of the Northern Highlands contribute to their sparse population. The whiskies from this region tend to be not quite as sweet as Speyside whiskies and a bit stronger and more full-bodied.

Campbeltown: This region was once home to the largest number of distillers, but through over-production and unsavory business tactics, it became associated with mediocre and cynical whisky production. Now that only two distilleries are left, I don't feel I can characterize the whiskies from Campbeltown. However, Springbank (one of the two that remain) produces some exceptional whisky.

Islay: Located on the southern coast of Scotland in view of Northern Ireland, Islay, (pronounced eye-laH) produces whiskies that are easily identified because of their intensity and very specific flavor profile. These whiskies are commonly described as briny, peaty, seaweedy, and medicinal. For some, their intensity may be a bit too much, but for those serious about their whisky, at least one favorite is likely to come from this region.

The Islands: Specifically, Skye, Mull, Orkney, and Jura. While the whiskies from these isles range in character from the heavily peated, briny Islay style to the stronger, full-bodied Northern Highlands style, all of these malts share a smoky aroma and flavor, and an oily mouth-feel.

The Lowlands: This region is the most industrialized and heavily populated of Scotland. Most Lowlands whisky is used for blending, although in recent years more of it has become available in individual distillery bottlings. The whiskies from this region are characterized by dryness and a rather volatile, alcoholic quality.

The French believe in a concept called *terroir.* Generally speaking, terroir means the specific attributes of a place, or to put it another way, a sense of place. The Chardonnay grape can be cul-

A view of the town of Craigellachie, from the Macallan Distillery.

Peat is not only used for making whisky. Pictured above is a warm peat fire at The Vaults, home of The Scotch Malt Whisky Society.

tivated and turned into wine in any number of locations over the globe, but, say the French, only Le Montrachet can "happen" on that particular 7.5 hectares within the communes of Puligny and Chassagne-Montrachet, in the Côte de Beaune, in the Côte d'Or, and in the region of Burgundy, in France. Can this idea, terroir, explain why Aberlour tastes so different from Tamdu? Or why

Lagavulin and Laphroaig, two distilleries from Islay just a stone's throw from each other, produce whiskies that smell and taste as different from each other as vanilla and licorice do?

The convergence of resources found in each region doubtless does influence its whisky. The chemicals in the water used to produce a particular whisky must play some role, creating more or less peatyness, more or less minerality. Likewise with the peating of the barley: how much peat is used, how much exposure of the barley to the smoke, and what other components are mixed in with the peat? Heather, for example, increases the perfumed quality of the smoke.

The shape, age, and condition of the stills also affect the outcome; longer-necked stills produce a lighter spirit, while shorter, squatter stills yield a heavier, more intense distillate. The mythology surrounding stills is so extreme that whenever a new still is required, whether because of expansion or to replace one no longer functioning, the new still is a replica of the other existing one, down to the patches and dents.

The whisky is further influenced by the skill of the still man—his sense of just when to draw off the best part of the spirit, his maniacal consistency and his possession of a nose able to discern 150 or more fragrances from a sample of whisky.

And, as I said before, last but not least, the wood and aging regimen are critical. I am inclined to believe that the attributes imparted to whisky from its long rest inside an oak barrel are significant. But more on this later.

*T*he Single Malt Difference

In the 1850s, Andrew Usher & Co. is reputed to have been the first merchant to make a blended whisky, thus launching a new era in the annals of whisky production. By definition, blended whisky is a proportion of malt whisky mixed with grain whisky. Grain whisky is a distillate that can be produced from a number of different grains including corn, wheat, and barley—both the malted (sprouted) and unmalted kinds. Grain whisky is produced in a patent still. This device, invented around 1830, differs from the pot still in that it can operate continuously, and does not need to be cleaned and recharged after each pass. While the patent still is tremendously efficient, the distillate

Haggis and whisky—the heart of a Robert Burns dinner held every January 25th.

Even though the barrels look identical, their contents are often unpredictable.

that it produces is a largely flavorless, colorless, odorless pure alcohol.

By contrast, single malt Scotch whisky is produced in a pot still from 100 percent malted barley, then aged in oak casks in Scotland for a minimum of three years, after which it has a proof of at least 40 percent alcohol. In addition, single malt Scotch whisky, in order to be called by that name, must be from a single distillery.

A blend of single malt whiskies—that is, a blend that contains no grain whisky—is called a vatted malt. Though not very popular in recent times, there seems to be a renewed interest in marketing this type of product.

In addition, as if this wasn't confusing enough, almost all distilleries will sell whisky in cask to private parties. A whisky society or other group of enthusiasts, or on a more commercial level, independent bottlers, will purchase whisky in cask and then bottle it themselves. Depending on the development of this whisky, it may be bottled immediately or allowed to continue aging for bottling at some future date. Besides The Scotch Malt Whisky Society, an organization with an enthusiastic membership worldwide, the two oldest independent bottling concerns are Gordon & MacPhail and Wm. Cadenhead. These companies bottle and market whiskies that otherwise would most likely never see the light of day. Unlike distillery-supervised bottling, these independent bottlings tend to come from single casks; consequently, there is quite a bit of variation from bottle to bottle. Not a bad thing at all, unless you eat all your meals at McDonald's and expect that kind of consistency in your whisky.

When a single malt is bottled at the distillery, it is generally a combination of several casks of similar age. This ensures a more consistent single malt. Most distilleries practice a cold filtration, so that the whisky will stay clear in the bottle. In addition, the whisky is rectified—that is, diluted with a percentage of water to achieve a uniform proof. By comparison, independent bottlers will bottle whisky from a single barrel, sometimes at cask strength, unrectified, and rarely cold filtered. Their goal: to create a bottled whisky that is as close as one can get to drinking right out of the cask.

There are pros and cons to these various types of bottlings, but they ultimately provide fodder for the endless debate on what makes single malt whisky so much fun to drink and discuss.

*A*ge Before Beauty

Before the turn of the century, single malt whisky was drunk pretty much un-aged. Collected at the distillery in a barrel, it was sold to a merchant who then bottled it as necessary. Around 1915, a governmental agency was formed to oversee the production of whisky and it decreed that whisky had to be aged in cask for a minimum of three years before it could be called whisky. Instead of using any old container to put the collected spirits in, distilleries were now compelled to use casks of a higher quality, as three years in a barrel that had previously held pickled

Cadenhead is a famous independent bottler—its shop in Edinburgh is well worth a trip. The store changes its selections daily based on the independent bottlings in stock—No bourbon drinkers allowed.

fish would have an impact on the whisky's flavor that might not be too nice. Casks that were made from French or American oak and used by Spanish sherry bodegas and Kentucky bourbon producers for aging and shipping became the Scotch distillers' vessels of choice. At this point in history, these barrels could be had for nominal prices for a variety of reasons, but mainly because it was cheaper for the owners of the bodegas and bourbon distilleries to sell them at the landing point than to ship them back empty. This turned out to be a boon for the Scots and their whisky, as several attributes of these barrels—the type of oak used, the process by which the barrels were constructed and the residual flavorings left from either the sherry or bourbon—proved to have a very positive effect on the aging whisky.

Most whisky is rectified, that is diluted with a little water before it goes into an oak cask. Whisky comes out of the still at around 70 percent alcohol, or 140 proof. It is rectified to approximately 63 percent alcohol when put in cask. At bottling, a further dilution occurs, 40 percent being the normal strength for European Economic Community countries, and 43 percent for whisky that is exported. With the growth of the independent bottling market (in which whisky is privately purchased in cask from the distiller and bottled elsewhere), one can also find "cask strength" bottlings. These range from 43 percent to more than 64 percent. Now many distilleries are experimenting with other types of oak barrels to finish their whisky, including those used in the aging of brandy, port and rum. In some cases, a whisky will spend eight years in a bourbon barrel—which tends to impart a lighter flavor than, say, a sherry barrel—and finish for six months to a year in a brandy barrel. I think that this development in whisky making is analogous to the chef who has just discovered seasonings from the Far East and is including them in his preparation of Western European dishes. Many try; few succeed.

As whisky ages, an exchange between the

liquid inside the barrel and the conditions outside the barrel occurs. Between 2 and 5 percent of the whisky in barrel evaporates into the atmosphere each year. The percentage varies, depending on the humidity in the cellar where the barrels are stored. The poetic name for this costly evaporation is known as the "angel's share." In addition, some feel that the characteristics of the environment in which it is aged can affect the whisky. For example, if the cellar is near the sea coast, the whisky will take on a briny or salty quality.

As whisky remains in its oak cask, it is transformed through the softening action of the oak tannins and other compounds found in the wood, as well as the flavors contained in the wood itself. As I have already noted, residual flavorings of bourbon, sherry or other liquids leave their marked characteristics.

The actual construction of the barrels can contribute to the whisky's flavor as well. When barrels are being made, the wood is cut into narrow planks called staves. These staves are air dried for a number of years to rid the wood of its most bitter tannin components. Next, the staves are soaked in water. An experienced cooper will then take each stave, and, holding it over a fire, bend it into the shape he needs for his barrel. This shaping process "toasts" the surface of the staves that will come in contact with the whisky. The "toast"

In the heart of Speyside is Dufftown. Rome had seven hills and Dufftown had seven stills—of which the most well-known today is Glenfiddich.

on a barrel, which can range anywhere from light to extra-dark, is therefore another source of flavor. The intensity of this characteristic varies depending on the intensity of the "toastedness" of the barrel.

Most whisky is released having been aged between eight and fifteen years. Common releases are: 8 year old, 10 year old, 12 year old, 14 year old, and 15 year old. Unless a whisky is from a single cask, in which case it will be identified as such, single malt Scotch whisky is the result of combining the contents of a number of casks that are generally, but not always, of the same age and the same distillery. The age stated on a bottle of whisky is the age of the youngest whisky contained in it. On the labels of older, rarer bottlings, one may find the date of distillation, the date of bottling and an age statement, e.g., 17 year old, 21 year old, etc. When an age statement is given, it is rounded to the lowest complete year that the whisky has been in cask. Sometimes a distillery will choose to quote a younger age statement or not give one at all.

Whisky does not inherently improve with age. (Just think of some of the people that you know). Certainly some rare, old expensive whiskies are much greater than their younger counterparts, but this tends to be the exception and not the rule. In our tasting we found that after 21 years, most whiskies begin to lose freshness and take on a rather musty, woody, flat character. Remember, this is just a general impression; we certainly found some very old whiskies to be very beautiful. About this question of age, first, when it comes to your own, always lie; secondly, when it comes to whisky, go out and taste for yourself and discover your own favorites.

Bottling

Interest outside of Scotland in single malt whisky has been increasing since the late 1970s. At the same time sales of blended whisky, while still the highest of the brown spirits, have been falling gradually; in the U.S. between '94 and '95, sales were down by 3.3%. For the same period, however, sales for single malts have increased by 14%. This upward trend shows no sign of abating. Distillers have been taking advantage of this trend by expanding the age range of their bottlings and independent bottlings have become more readily available. Various firms, which include Gordon & MacPhail and Cadenhead, as well as a number of clubs and societies-including The Scotch Malt Whisky Society will purchase whisky in cask from the distillery, store it and bottle it themselves. Consequently, at this point in time it is virtually impossible to have a definitive book containing all of the whiskies available in the world, as that number is constantly changing.

What we have done in our book is presented you with a general overview including blended, distillery, and independent bottlings. The relative alcoholic strength of the different bottlings, as previously stated, works like this: Distillery bottlings are at 40% alcohol (80 proof) when sold in any member country of the EEC, 43% (86 proof) when sold on the export market. Independent bottlings may be sold at "cask" strength. This number can vary from 43% (86 proof) to 67% (134 proof). When reading the tasting notes, the sample used will always be identified. Distillery bottlings tend to be much more consistent than independent bottlings. Distilleries will blend various casks of single malt whisky in order to achieve

what they feel is the supreme expression of their product. Independent bottlings are from single casks, and these casks exhibit quite a bit of variation from one another. This is by no means a bad thing, but it would be unfair to judge a whisky from just one taste from one independent bottle. We found it to be most rewarding to compare the distilleries bottling against an independent whenever both samples were available. With the exception of certain private society bottlings, distillery name and age and strength statements are in evidence on the label. In some cases, casks are purchased from defunct distilleries. The independent bottles will be the last samples ever available. Ardbeg, Dallas Dhu, and North Port, samples of which have been included in the book are now all closed. Thanks to the efforts of these groups, the memory of some of the closed distilleries will live on for a while longer.

The Official Tasting

Samples were collected from a variety of sources—distributors, producers, independent bottlers—all helpful people—a guest list was devised to include: people from the trade, food professionals, interested amateurs, friends from the publishing and photography world (notorious scotch drinkers, both), and a few civilians. Tasting sheets were designed, a venue found, hors d'oeuvres selected, invitations delivered, instant scotch party. Many of the quotes that you will see reproduced in the tasting notes section of the book came from that event. Also, some of you may wonder why the bottles pictured are at different levels. The answer is, what is Scotch for after all, if not to drink, so that was what we did. Clever readers might find a clue as to which whiskies were more favored than others just by looking at the pictures, but don't forget that during the arduous task of writing this book I found it most inspiring to have a dram now and then.

The Tasting at the JUdson Grill
New York City

How to Use This Book

I had met my editor for lunch sometime ago and pitched her an idea I had about writing and taking photographs for a book about wine. We talked for a while and she said that she thought it was a pretty good idea, but at the moment they just didn't need a book about wine. Nice lunch, some decent wine, and I was glad that she thought my idea was interesting. What she hadn't told me that day was that they did need a book about Scotch whisky. Now most of the other people who have written books about Scotch whisky are pretty much obsessed with Scotch, with Scotland, and with whisky. I'm pretty obsessed too, but I'm obsessed with wine. I'm in the wine trade, I write about wine, create wine lists for restaurants, drink it, sell it, taste it, talk about it, teach about it, drink it, think about it, and, even take pictures of it. But Scotch...?!!

As my research and tasting explorations brought me deeper into the world of single malt whisky I found, not surprisingly, that as much complexity, intellectual stimulation, and sensual pleasure that I had discovered in the world of wine was happily awaiting me in the world of whisky. Plus the additional pleasure of meeting a whole new cast of characters—the "whisky people."

For all of you that drink blended whisky— 9,450,000 liters worth in 1996—I hope that some of the pleasure that we found in trying different kinds of single malts will entice you to explore on your own and compare your tasting sensations with ours.

As I say, ad nauseam, when I talk about wine, it's not what someone else says is the best, it's what you love. Taste with friends and argue about which Scotch is best. This is great stuff.

Single Malt & Scotch Whisky

Tasting Form

Table no. _____   **Brand** _____

Please answer the questions by marking on the bar graphs below:

Body

What is the weight or mouth feel of this whisky?

Heaviest _____|_____ **Ligh**

How intense or subtle are the aromas in this whisky?

Fullest _____|_____ **Lig**

How complex and how powerful are the flavors in this whisky?

Strong _____|_____

Other comments: _____

_____

_____

Circle as many or as few aroma and flavor characteristics as necessary:

Aroma

| Floral | Fruity | Spicy | Hot | Earthy | Oily | Nut |

Flavor

| Sweet | Salty | Peppery | Smoky | Sour | Caramel | Va |
| Tobacco | Coffee | Sulphur | Anise | Peach | Citrus | M |

Other: _____

Please elaborate on aroma and/or flavor if necessary: _____

_____

Please record your personal impressions and reactions: _____

_____

_____

Single Malt & Scotch Whisky
Tasting Form

ble no. **5**   Brand **Edradour**

e answer the questions by marking on the bar graphs below:

Body

s the weight or mouth feel of this whisky?

viest ————|————————|———————— **Lightest**

tense or subtle are the aromas in this whisky?

est ————————————||——————— **Lightest**

nplex and how powerful are the flavors in this whisky?

ng ————————|—|———————— **Light**

r comments: _____

_____
_____
_____

any or as few aroma and flavor characteristics as necessary:

Aroma

Fruity   (Spicy)   (Hot)   (Earthy)   Oily   Nutty   Grassy

Flavor

Salty   (Peppery)   (Smoky)   Sour   (Caramel)   Vanilla   (Peaty)
Coffee   Sulphur   Anise   Peach   Citrus   Mint   Woody

te on aroma and/or flavor if necessary: _____

our personal impressions and reactions: _____

ooth & spicy, finish not too explosive!

*S*ingle Malt
Whisky Brands

ABERLOUR

ESTD 1879

ABERLOUR
GLENLIVET
DISTILLERY

SPEYSIDE
MALT AGED
TEN YEARS

SINGLE HIGHLAND MALT
SCOTCH WHISKY

AGED **10** YEARS

750 ml

DISTILLED AND BOTTLED IN SCOTLAND
ABERLOUR GLENLIVET DISTILLERY CO. LTD.
ABERLOUR SPEYSIDE

43%
Alc/Vol

0753

*A**berlour*

aber-lower

Highland (Speyside)

AGE WHEN BOTTLED: 10 year old, 21 year old, "100" year old and Antique.

STRENGTH: 10 year old, 40%; 21 year old and Antique, 43%; 100 year old, 57%.

Aberlour was founded in 1826, but its label reads 1879. This latter date reflects the year the distillery was rebuilt after a devastating fire. Pernod-Ricard, a French conglomerate, now owns the distillery, and in addition to modernizing the facilities, it has launched a massive advertising push at home. As a result, most of Aberlour's single malt bottlings are sold in France. Much of the distillery's production is used for blending.

"Smooth yet rich; a pleasure to drink."

AROMAS: Spicy, hot, grassy, floral.

FLAVORS: Peppery, caramel, toffee, medium to full body, long finish.

Aberfeldy

Highland (Southern)

AGE WHEN BOTTLED: 15 year old.

STRENGTH: 43%.

Built by the sons of the famous blender John Dewar in the 1890s, this distillery is situated in a beautiful woodland, which is home to a fine family of red squirrels whose likeness is emblazoned on the Aberfeldy label. Mostly used for blending (Dewar's), some are available in both independent and distillery bottlings.

"Smells like vanilla ice cream."
"Rich and pleasant."

AROMAS: Nutty, fragrant, oaky notes.

FLAVORS: Rich, a bit sweet, smooth finish.

*A*llt-A-Bhannie

ahlt-a-bane or olt-a-vane

Highland (Speyside)

AGE WHEN BOTTLED: 12 year old.

STRENGTH: 56%.

Although it is one of the newer distilleries extant, dating from 1975, Allt-A-Bhannie was built in traditional style by the Seagram Company. All of its large (1 million gallons plus) output is used for blending.

"A spicy little dram."
"Rather perky."

AROMAS: Coffee, toffee, slightly hot.

FLAVORS: A bit smoky, hot, sweetish, a touch sour in the finish.

*A*rdbeg

Islay

AGE WHEN BOTTLED: Various
ages, all independent bottlings.

STRENGTH: Most bottlings, 40%.

Prior to 1815, when the distillery was officially
recognized by excise officials, this site was used for
illicit distilling. Sheltered, with access to lots of peat,
barley, and good water, Ardbeg is a perfect example
of an island distillery. The bulk of its whisky has
been used for blending, but now Ardbeg is also
available as a single malt from a variety of
independent bottlers. At the moment, the distillery
is not operational. Tasting notes refer to a 20 year old
Gordon & MacPhail bottling.

"Like a fist to the jaw."
"Best of the tasting."

AROMAS: Earthy, oily, spicy, a bit burnt.

FLAVORS: Strong, salty, woody, quite layered.
A whisky for aficionados.

Ardmore

Highland (Speyside)

AGE WHEN BOTTLED: Only independent bottlings are available.

STRENGTH: 18 year old, 59.3%.

One of the largest distilleries in Scotland, Ardmore was built by William Teacher in the 1890s. Expanded and modernized in the 1950s, this distillery produces the whisky that goes into Teacher's blended whisky. All available bottlings are independent.

"Light and flashy, but not much substance."

AROMAS: A little smoky.

FLAVORS: Grassy, slight bite.

*A*uchentoshan

awk-en-taw-shen or och-en-to-shen

Lowland

AGE WHEN BOTTLED: 10 year old, 21 year old.

STRENGTH: 10 year old, 40%; 21 year old, 43%.

The origins of this distillery are a bit sketchy;
the earliest record of ownership dates back to 1825.
Damaged during World War II, the distillery was
later rebuilt and modernized. Located right on the
dividing line between Lowland and Highland, the
distillery sits on the Lowland side but uses peat and
water from the Highland side. Usually whisky is
distilled twice, but in the case of Auchentoshan, a
third trip through the still is added. The resulting
very smooth whisky is used as an ingredient in
various blended whiskies. One may tour this
distillery. Tasting notes refer to the 10 year old.

"Tastes expensive."

AROMAS: Light, fresh, grassy, lemon.

FLAVORS: Light, clean, citrus, honey, vanilla.

*A*ultmore

Highland (Speyside)

AGE WHEN BOTTLED: 12 year old.

STRENGTH: 43%.

Built in the mid 1850s, Aultmore possesed two
steam-powered stills until the 1970s, when it doubled
in size and modernized its energy source. Originally
called the "Oban and Aultmore-Glenlivet Distillery,"
the name was shortened when a map was consulted
and it became apparent that Aultmore was a bit
distant from the eponymous glen. Most of its
production is used for blending.

"Pleasant. I liked it."

AROMAS: Light, faint nose, bit of fruit.

FLAVORS: Smooth, dry, rather simple, pleasant.

PRODUCT OF SCOTLAND

BALBLAIR

Single Highland
Malt Scotch
Whisky
UNBLENDED   POT STILL

750ml   *years old* **10** *years old*   40%alc/vol
(80Proof)

TRADEMARK OF PROPRIETORS
Balblair Distillery Company Ltd
Edderton by Tain

SPECIALLY SELECTED, PRODUCED, MATURED & BOTTLED BY
AND UNDER THE RESPONSIBILITY OF
GORDON & MACPHAIL
ELGIN SCOTLAND REGD. BOTTLER

*B*alblair

Highland (Speyside)

AGE WHEN BOTTLED: 5 year old and 10 year old (15 year old, independent bottling).

STRENGTH: 5 year old and 10 year old, 40%.

Balblair is one of the oldest distilleries in Scotland, originating between 1750 and 1790. It is located in an area that has seen much whisky production, licensed and otherwise, due to its close proximity to excellent sources of peat and fresh water. Most of Balblair whisky is used for blending, with a high percentage being incorporated into Ballantine's blended Scotch whisky. Tasting notes refer to the 10 year old.

"Pretty easy to drink, slightly nutty."

AROMAS: Smoky, sweet, nutty.

FLAVORS: Clean, a bit simple, smoky finish.

67

*B*alvenie

Highland (Speyside)

AGE WHEN BOTTLED: 10 year old and 12 year old.

STRENGTH: 43%.

Built by William Grant in the 1890s, this distillery stands next to Glenfiddich. Balvenie still has its own maltings and also shares a steam heat source with its more famous neighbor, presumably in exchange for some barrels of Balvenie. Tasting notes refer to 12 year old.

"Strong, intense, perfumy"

AROMAS: Floral, high-toned nose.

FLAVORS: Rich hints of honey, a long layered finish.

Ben Nevis

Highland (Western)

AGE WHEN BOTTLED: 19 year old, 21 year old, 26 year old.

STRENGTH: Strengths vary from cask to cask.

Ben Nevis was founded by "Long John" Macdonald in 1825. It was passed to generations of the Macdonald family until it was bought by a subsidiary of Seager, Evans & Whitbread & Co, Ltd in 1981. The changing of hands ceased after a coffey and four pot stills were added. Finally Ben Nevis was sold to Nikka, a Japanese company, in 1989.

"A very special treat to drink before or after dinner."

AROMAS: Fruity and peaty.

FLAVORS: Full, nutty, earthy, and peaty.

*B*enriach

Highland

AGE WHEN BOTTLED:
10 year old.

STRENGTH: 43%.

Founded in the 1890s, Benriach
had a short life. The distillery
closed in 1900 and remained that
way for more than half a century.
Since its reopening in 1965, a large
portion of its production goes
toward blending and a smaller
part is independently bottled.

"Strong, but easy to drink."

AROMAS: Fruity, spicy, hot.

FLAVORS: Sweet, peach, caramel,
lighter finish.

BENRIACH DISTILLERY
EST. 1898
A SINGLE
PURE HIGHLAND MALT
Scotch Whisky

Benriach Distillery, in the heart of the Highlands,
still malts its own barley. The resulting whisky has
a unique and attractive delicacy

PRODUCED AND BOTTLED BY THE

BENRIACH
DISTILLERY C?
ELGIN, MORAYSHIRE, SCOTLAND, IV30 3SJ
Distilled and Bottled in Scotland
PRODUCE OF SCOTLAND

AGED 10 YEARS

IMPORTED BY THE BENRIACH DISTILLING CO, NY, NY

750 ML.   ALC. 43% BY VOL.

71

*B*enromach

Highland (Speyside)

AGE WHEN BOTTLED: 12 year old.

STRENGTH: 40%.

Since its inception in 1898, Benromach has changed ownership more than a few times. In 1983, DCL, the owner at the time, shut a number of distilleries in its portfolio, including Benromach. The distillery was purchased in 1992 by Gordon & MacPhail and was scheduled to reopen in the fall of 1997. Benromach has a reputation for producing a clean, medium peated, lighter style of Highland whisky. Tasting notes refer to a 12 year old, 40% Gordon & MacPhail bottling.

"Good, long spicy finish."

AROMAS: Sweet on the nose; a little smoky and peaty.

FLAVORS: Nutty, exotic spice, cinnamon.

*B*ladnoch

Lowland

AGE WHEN BOTTLED: No longer distilling, various independent bottlings: 10 year old, 11 year old, 15 year old, 16 year old.

STRENGTH: 43%.

The southernmost of all distilleries, Bladnoch has been opened and closed a number of times during its long history. The final closing occurred in 1994, and the site is now used as tourist center. Once the remaining stocks have been bottled and sold, Bladnoch will be no more.

"Like butter, ya know?"

AROMAS: Smoky, caramel, oily.

FLAVORS: Heavy, peaty, tangy, rich.

*B*owmore

Islay

AGE WHEN BOTTLED: 10 year old, 12 year old, 15 year old, 17 year old, 21 year old, 22 year old, 25 year old and 30 year old, Legend (no age given).

STRENGTH: 10 year old, 12 year old, Legend, 40%; 15 year old, 21 year old, 22 year old, 30 year old, 43%; 25 year old Black Bowmore (a rare cask bottling), 50%.

The oldest distillery on this island, Bowmore was established in 1779. Long owned by Morrison Bowmore Distillers, whose holdings include Auchentoshan and Glen Garioch, Bowmore was sold in 1997 to Suntory of Japan. Even before that sale, however, much of this whisky went to Japan. Bowmore malts most of its own barley. The traditional malting barns with pagoda-shaped ventilators on their roofs now have a new Far Eastern resonance. Tasting notes refer to 17 year old.

"Yum." (Stated twice by different tasters.)

AROMAS: Musky, earthy, nutty aromas. Beautiful, rich color.

FLAVORS: Dry, charcoal, moderate peat, smoky, a touch bitter, very complex.

Brora

Highland (Speyside)

AGE WHEN BOTTLED: 18 year old sample (private bottling).

STRENGTH: 60.3%.

Brora distillery was founded in 1819, and was situated next to the Brora coalfield which provided ready power for the distilling process. In 1896, James Ainslie & Co. took over Brora and rebuilt the distillery just a mile from its original site. DCL then acquired a large holding in Brora; the Clynelish Distillery Co. was formed; and Brora was renamed as Clynelish (klein-leash). (See Clynelish.) In 1925, DCL gained complete control and built a new malt whisky distillery next to Clynelish called Brora that operated until 1968. Brora was closed in 1983 and was transformed into a tourist attraction. Tasting notes refer to an 18 year old sample.

"Very pleasant"

AROMAS: Sweet, vanilla.

FLAVORS: Clean, fresh, fruity.

The rolling Highlands

*B*ruichladdich

brew-ich-laddie

Islay

AGE WHEN BOTTLED: 10 year old, 15 year old, 21 year old.

STRENGTH: 10 year old and 15 year old, 40%; 21 year old, 43%.

Closed since 1995, Bruichladdich was built right on the sea. Most Islay whiskies are very heavy and peaty, but Bruichladdich is a much lighter malt. According to some experts, this is because the water source for the distillery is an inland reservoir which contains much softer water. Tasting notes refer to 15 year old.

"Nice, even, very mellow."

AROMAS: Nutty, sweet, light, a touch peaty.

FLAVORS: Mellow, smoky, a bit sweet, intense, rich finish.

Bunnahabhain

boon-a-ha-ven

Islay

AGE WHEN BOTTLED: 12 year old and occasional independent bottlings.

STRENGTH: 12 year old, 43%.

The name Bunnahabhain means the mouth of the river. This distillery, situated on the northeast coast of Islay, produces a moderately "iodiney" style of Islay whisky. Bunnahabhain is used for blending in The Famous Grouse.

"Really briny and fresh, tastes like the sea. A lot of spice in the finish."

AROMAS: Floral and fresh, with touches of hazelnut and earth.

FLAVORS: Smoky, peppery, hint of wood, a distinct coffee note.

aged **12** years

"Westering Home..."

Bunnahabhain

SINGLE ISLAY MALT SCOTCH WHISKY

PRODUCT OF SCOTLAND

THE BUNNAHABHAIN DISTILLERY COMPANY.
BUNNAHABHAIN, ISLE OF ISLAY, SCOTLAND. BOTTLED IN SCOTLAND

Sole U.S.A. Distributor,
Rémy Amérique, Inc.,
New York, N.Y.

43% alc/vol

750 ml.

*C*aol *I*la

Coal-eel-a or kaal-eela (depends on who you ask)

Islay

AGE WHEN BOTTLED: 12 year old, 13 year old, 14 year old, 15 year old, 17 year old, 19 year old, 20 year old, 21 year old, and various independent bottlings.

STRENGTH: 40%, 43% and 60%—strengths vary with years.

Caol Ila is Gaelic for Sound of Islay. This distillery was completely rebuilt in the early 1970s. Almost all of the whisky is used for blending, but the occasional independent bottling shows up. (Tasting notes refer to 14 year old 40% Gordon & MacPhail bottling.)

"Excellent accompaniment to a fine Cuban cigar."

AROMAS: Earthy, peaty, a touch grassy.

FLAVORS: Earthy, salty, smoky, longish finish.

Caperdonich

Highland (Speyside)

AGE WHEN BOTTLED: 16 year old.

STRENGTH: 40%.

Originally called Glen Grant 2, the distillery was built in 1897 as an adjunct to Glen Grant. The new facility's production was piped into Glen Grant until the turn of the century. The distillery was closed until 1965, when it was expanded and renamed Caperdonich. Its output is mostly availble as independent bottlings.

"Reminded me of a candy bar."

AROMAS: Chocolate, caramel, and burnt sugar aroma.

FLAVORS: Sweet, woody, a bit of smoke on the palate.

Cardhu

Highland (Speyside)

AGE WHEN BOTTLED: 12 year old.

STRENGTH: 40%.

An old distillery, Cardhu means black rock in Gaelic. Modernized in the 1960s, the bulk of its whisky is used in Johnnie Walker Black and Red Label blends. On its own, Cardhu is light in color and shows hardly any peat character.

"Zippy little Scotch."

AROMAS: Light, faintly earthy, citrus.

FLAVORS: Fresh, lively, a touch of wood and smoke.

Clynelish

klyn-leesh

Highland (Northern)

AGE WHEN BOTTLED: 14 year old, 15 year old, various independent bottlings (12 year old Glen Haven bottling tasted).

STRENGTH: 14 year old and 15 year old, 43%; independent bottlings range in strength; 12 year old tasted, 61%.

Clynelish (also see Brora) originally opened in 1819 as a brewery and was converted to a distillery soon after. This distillery was originally named Brora, but in 1912, because of a change of ownership, the distillery was renamed Clynelish. In 1925 another distillery was built next door and given the old name of Brora. In 1969 Clynelish reopened housed in the former mash house of Brora. Its production from the mash house was stenciled as "Brora" on the casks, but sold under the name of Clynelish for fillings. The distillery subsequently ceased operation in May, 1983, was closed, and has now become a visitor center.

"Man, that is intense."
"Very strong but very nice."
"Very explosive."

AROMAS: Peaty, medicinal, smoky.

FLAVORS: Smoke, heavy peat.

Cragganmore

Highland (Speyside)

AGE WHEN BOTTLED: 12 year old.

STRENGTH: 40%.

This distillery was established in 1869 by the very experienced John Smith. This Mr. Smith had managed several distilleries including Macallan and Glenlivet prior to striking out on his own. The distillery was one of the first to make use of a nearby railway link, perhaps one of the reasons that the bulk of the production has always been used for blending. In recent years, this whisky has become one of the United Distillers' Classic Malts, and as such, is now widely available. The stills used are quite old fashioned in their design.

"Strong, but I like it."

AROMAS: Dry, little hot, smoky, hint of fruit.

FLAVORS: Medium to heavy body, long, spicy, bit of vanilla.

40%alc

The Best of Speysi...

MALT

CRAGGANMO

SINGLE HIGHLAND

AGED **12** YEARS

Scotch Whisky

SOLE DISTRIBUTOR IN USA,
SCHIEFFELIN & SOMERSET CO.
NEW YORK, N.Y.
PRODUCT OF SCOTLAND

SPECIALLY BOTTLED IN SCOTLAND FOR THE
CRAGGANMORE DISTILLERY, BALLINDALLOCH, BANFF...

RARE

85

Dallas Dhu

Highland (Speyside)

AGE WHEN BOTTLED: 10 year old, 12 year old, 17 year old, 20 year old, 30 year old (all independent bottlings).

STRENGTH: Various strengths.

Closed for business now, this distillery is run as a tourist attraction. Visit it to see what things were like around the turn of the century. Various independent bottlings from old casks are available, although not too readily. Tasting notes refer to 12 year old.

"Really powerful and interesting."

AROMAS: Hot, oily, nutty, earthy, mushroomy.

FLAVORS: Earthy, woody, syrupy mouthfeel, caraway, citrus, intense.

87

Dalmore

Highland (Speyside)

AGE WHEN BOTTLED: 12 year old.

STRENGTH: 40%, numerous independent bottlings at various strengths.

This distillery was founded in 1839 and operated continously until World War I. At that time the facility was retooled for the production of naval mines. Modernized in 1966, it continues to use several of the stills dating back to 1874. Most all of its output goes for blending.

"Very pretty whisky."

AROMAS: Soft, fruity, light nose.

FLAVORS: Full, a bit peaty, smooth, rich finish.

Dalwhinnie

Highland

AGE WHEN BOTTLED: 15 year old.

STRENGTH: 43%

Gaelic for meeting place, Dalwhinnie is situated on a rail spur, with abundant peat and fresh water sources and the highest elevation of any distillery in Scotland. Built in 1897 the distillery went through a variety of bankruptcies, purchases, and fires until it finally stabilized in 1938. Although most of its output is used for blending, this malt is now available as part of the Classic Malt series.

"Clean, very fresh."

AROMAS: Light, fresh, a hint of peat.

FLAVORS: A bit sweet, floral, honied, medium length.

Deanston

Highland (Southern)

AGE WHEN BOTTLED: 12 year old, 17 year old, 25 year old, a few independent bottlings.

STRENGTH: 12 year old, 17 year old and 25 year old, 40%.

Deanston was founded in 1965, which makes this distillery a relative newcomer. It sits on the site of an old textile mill and is named after a nearby town. The new owners use unpeated barley for the whisky. Tasting notes refer to 17 year old.

"Very heady."

AROMAS: Nutty and vanilla aromas.

FLAVORS: Smoky, medium peatyness, nutty, sweetish finish.

Dufftown-Glenlivet

Highland (Speyside)

AGE WHEN BOTTLED: 12 year old, various independent bottlings.

STRENGTH: 43%, numerous independent bottlings of various strengths.

The town of Dufftown has a long-standing reputation for producing some of the finest whisky in Scotland. Dufftown-Glenlivet is another distillery that felt compelled, like so many of its neighbors, to add Glenlivet to its name. The distillery was built in 1887 and purchased by the famous blenders, Arthur Bell & Sons, in 1933. Since then, most of this whisky has gone into a variety of Bell's blends. In 1974, Bell built a sister distillery for Dufftown called Pittvaich-Glenlivet. The idea was to increase production without compromising quality, an admirable notion. The new distillery copied down to the last detail the pot stills from Dufftown-Glenlivet. Tasting notes refer to 12 year old.

"Tastes familiar, like perfect Scotch."

AROMAS: Fruity, with notes of apple and pear.

FLAVORS: Lightish, clean, fresh, a bit floral.

Aged 10 years

THE
EDRADOUR

EST. 1825
*The smallest distillery
in Scotland*

750ml   43% ALC/VOL

*Single Highland Malt
Scotch Whisky*

GLENFORRES GLENLIVET DISTILLERY CO. LTD.
EDRADOUR DISTILLERY, PITLOCHRY, SCOTLAND

PRODUCT OF SCOTLAND

The Edradour

Highland (Speyside)

AGE WHEN BOTTLED: 10 year old, various independent bottlings.

STRENGTH: 10 year old, 43%; independent bottlings at various strengths.

Edradour, the smallest distillery in Scotland, functions as if it were still operating in the 19th century. The entire enterprise is run by four people and almost everything is done by hand. Appointments for tours are necessary; if you want to travel back in time, Edradour is a good place to visit.

"Smooth and spicy, finish not too explosive."

AROMAS: Spicy, hot, earthy nose.

FLAVORS: Peppery, peaty, smoky, hints of tobacco and caramel.

Glen Garioch

Glen-gee-ree

Highland (Eastern)

AGE WHEN BOTTLED: 12 year old, 15 year old, 21 year old.

STRENGTH: 12 year old, 40%; all others, 43%.

One of the oldest distilleries in Scotland, Glen Garioch has records that go as far back as 1785. Well situated with access to abundant sources of peat and fresh water, Glen Garioch also cleverly uses waste heat from the malting and distilling process to grow tomatoes in greenhouses on the property. Some of this whisky finds its way into Vat 69, as well as other blends. Tasting notes refer to 12 year old.

"Peaty and nice."

AROMAS: Flowery and smoky, pleasant aromas.

FLAVORS: Peppery, with a hint of clove, some peat and smoke.

96

AGED FIFTEEN YEARS

GLEN®
GARIOCH

HIGHLAND
Single Malt
SCOTCH WHISKY

DISTILLED & BOTTLED IN SCOTLAND

MORRISON'S GLEN GARIOCH DISTILLERY

ml   43% Alc./ 97

Glen Grant

Highland (Speyside)

AGE WHEN BOTTLED: 5 year old and 10 year old; rare independent bottling—12 year old, 21 year old, 25 year old, 30 year old and 40 year old.

STRENGTH: 5 year old, 40%; 10 year old, 43%.

Started in 1840, Glen Grant has been quite successful, and with the exception of a short period around the turn of the century, has continued to expand, producing whisky all year long. Very popular in Italy and fairly hard to find elsewhere, Glen Grant turns up independently bottled in various strengths and ages. Tasting notes refer to 5 year old.

"Absolutely my favorite."

AROMAS: Light, fruity aromas.

FLAVORS: A touch sweet, very dry.

FROM THE HEATH COVERED   MOUNTAINS OF SCOTIA I COME

YEARS
30
OLD

HIGHLAND   WHISKY

MALT SCOTCH

PRODUCE OF SCOTLAND.
GLEN GRANT
DISTILLED & BOTTLED IN SCOTLAND

750ml

ESTABLISHED
1840

40%alc/vol
(80Proof)

J.& J.GRANT
OF
GLEN GRANT
DISTILLERY

ROTHES

Bottled by :
GORDON & MACPHAIL
Wine & Spirit Merchants,
Elgin.

G. CORNWALL & SONS LTD
ABERDEEN

Glen Keith

Highland (Speyside)

AGE WHEN BOTTLED: 10 year old.

STRENGTH: 43%.

The first new distillery in Scotland in the twentieth century, Glen Keith is also one of the most modern. The distillery uses gas-fired instead of coal-fired stills, and the whole operation is computerized. Mostly used for blending by Chivas Brothers, it is now available in a Seagram's bottling.

"Delicious"

AROMAS: Nutty, oily, a touch oaky.

FLAVORS: Soft, smooth, citrus, rich finish.

PRODUCE OF SCOTLAND

GLENKEITH

SINGLE HIGHLAND MALT
SCOTCH WHISKY

Distilled before

1983

750 ML.

ALC. 43%
BY VOL.

A fragrant whisky
from the heart of
the Highlands.
GLEN KEITH
is prized by
experts for its
purity and depth
of flavour

GLEN KEITH
is matured for
more than ten
years in oak casks.
The whisky is then
bottled under the
supervision of our
Head Distiller

The pool of the Salmon

The Glen Keith distillery stands beside the fast-flowing river Isla,
above a deep pool where wild salmon swim and leap. The Gaelic name is
linne a bhradan. Here, nature is unspoilt, the air and the water pure and
sweet. It is in the very heart of Scotch Whisky country.

IMPORTED BY THE GLEN KEITH DISTILLING CO, NY, NY.

BOTTLED IN SCOTLAND

20KF802

Glen Ord

Highland (Northern)

AGE WHEN BOTTLED: 12 year old (occasional independent).

STRENGTH: 40%.

In the early nineteenth century numerous distilleries existed in Scotland, but in 1924, Glenlivet, also in the Highland, was the first to be licensed. The wave of legalization that followed sent many illegal distilleries on the straight and narrow, and many shut-down facilities were relicensed and transformed for new production. Glen Ord, for one, built on the site of an illegal distillery, was licensed in 1838. Still using water to power some of the distillery operations until the 1960s, Glen Ord is now quite a large enterprise. This distillery mixes heather in with the peat to be used during the drying process.

"Cool and smooth, easy to drink."

AROMAS: Nutty, grassy, a hint of floral.

FLAVORS: Light, citrus, peach, very dry finish.

103

THE GLENROTHES DISTILLERY

SAMPLE ROOM

CHARACTER: *Delicate, peaty undertones.*

CHECKED: *J.C. Stevens* DATE: 4/7/84.

APPROVED: *R.H. Fenwick* DATE: 8.9.95.

Distilled and Bottled in Scotland. Berry Bros. & Rudd Ltd, 3 St James's Street, London.

DISTILLED IN
1979
BOTTLED IN 1996
17 YEARS OLD

CGF041

43% Alc./Vol. SCOTCH WHISKY 750 ml.
PRODUCT OF SCOTLAND

Glen Rothes

Highland (Speyside)

AGE WHEN BOTTLED: 15 year old and various independent bottlings.

STRENGTH: 15 year old, 43%; independent bottlings in a range of strengths.

Almost all of Glen Rothes is used for blending Famous Grouse and Cutty Sark. A large commercial concern, this distillery produces over 1 million gallons of whisky annually.

"A find."
"My favorite."
"A whisky with deep, complex aromas and flavors."

AROMAS: Complex, spicy, light peat, nutty.

FLAVORS: Caramel, buttery, vanilla, sweet, smoky finish.

Glen Scotia

glen-sko-sha

Campbeltown

AGE WHEN BOTTLED: 8 year old, 12 year old, 14 year old, 17 year old and independent bottlings at various ages and strengths.

STRENGTH: 12 year old, 43%; all other years, 40%.

In the nineteenth century this town possessed the greatest concentration of distilleries in all of Scotland; now, only two still produce whisky. Because its distilleries sold lots of mediocre whisky for a long time, the name Campbeltown became associated with a less than quality product, and the whisky world is nothing if not a meritocracy. Opened and closed a number of times during the past 100 years, Glen Scotia has been closed since 1994. The distillery is rumored to be haunted. (Tasting notes refer to 21 year old 40%.)

"Very heady."

AROMAS: Sweet, fruity, floral.

FLAVORS: Heavy, oily, peaty, fat.

*G*lendronach

Highland (Speyside)

AGE WHEN BOTTLED: 12 year old, 18 year old, 20 year old; also divided by wood treatment. Traditional bottlings use sherry and oak barrels, and others use just sherry casks.

STRENGTH: 10 year old, 40%; independent bottlings at various strengths.

Traditional elements such as floor maltings, coal-fired stills, etc. abound, even though the distillery was modernized and expanded in the late 1960s. Much of this whisky goes into the blended Scotch, Teacher's. Tasting notes refer to 12 year old sherry cask.

"Quite a shining Scotch. Very polished and round."

AROMAS: Fruity, sweet, nutty citrus-orange peel.

FLAVORS: Toffee, coffee, smoky, caramel finish. A good example of just how much the wood contributes to the whisky's character.

Glenfarclas

Highland (Speyside)

AGE WHEN BOTTLED: 10 year old, 12 year old, 15 year old, 21 year old, 25 year old, "105" (cask strength).

STRENGTH: 10 year old, 40%; 12, 21 and 25 year old, 43%; 15 year old, 46%; cask strength, 60%.

For five generations, this distillery has been privately owned by the Grant family. Modernized twice, first in the 1960s, and again in the 1980s, Glenfarclas is a large, up-to-date facility—a very nice place to visit. As the first distillery to commercially bottle "cask strength" whisky, Glenfarclas started a trend that has become de riguer for single malt enthusiasts. Glenfarclas now ages all its spirits exclusively in sherry casks.

25 year old: "Delicious and important."

AROMAS: 12 year old: nutty, grassy; 17 year old: floral, nutty, grassy; 21 year old: fruity, sweet, vanilla, nutty; 25 year old: fruity, oily, earthy, nutty; 105 year old: hot, intense, spicy.

FLAVORS: 12 year old: sweet, light, simple; 17 year old: hot, very long, woody, a bit smoky; 21 year old: smoky, quite woody, meaty, earthy, dark flavors; 25 year old: sweet, caramel, toffee, vanilla, tobacco, smoky, very smooth; 105 year old: hot, spicy, peppery, dry. Perfect examples of characteristics related to the aging process. Some love the freshness and bite of younger whisky; others, the intensity of strong alcohol content, while still others love the cognac or madeira-like qualities associated with highly aged whiskies.

Glengoyne

Highland (Southern)

AGE WHEN BOTTLED: 10 year old, 12 year old, 17 year old, 25 year old.

STRENGTH: 10 year old, 40% and 43%; 12 year old and 17 year old, 43%; 25 year old, 47%.

Glengoygne is located directly on the imaginary line that divides the Highlands from the Lowlands. After being owned and operated for over 100 years by the Lang family, the distillery was purchased in 1965 and completely modernized by Robertson & Baxter. The whisky is made by using an unpeated malt and spring water that contains no peat. Most likely, this whisky is the least peaty of all single malts. As these whiskies age, however, they darken in color and become more layered and complex on the nose and palate. A large amount of this whisky is used for blending. Local legend has it that Rob Roy hid in a hollow tree near the distillery to avoid being captured.

"A whisky with a very nice feeling."

AROMAS: 10 year old: very light, fresh, clean a touch of mint and fruit; 17 year old: floral, fruity, nutty.

FLAVORS: 10 year old: a bit sweet, light, citrus, a touch of pepper in the finish, 17 year old: sweet, caramel, vanilla, woody on the finish.

113

Glenkinchie

glen-kin-chee

Lowland

AGE WHEN BOTTLED: 10 year old.

STRENGTH: 40%.

Glenkinchie

THE EDINBURGH MALT
LOWLAND SCOTCH WHISKY

Glenkinchie Distillery was established in 1837 by John and George Rate. It is situated beside the Kinchie Burn in the heart of East Lothian farmland. Over the gently rolling hills around Glenkinchie, some of the finest barley is grown.

Glenkinchie Lowland Malt Whisky has a light delicate nose and a fresh clean aroma; the finish is smooth, with a subtle hint of dryness. A truly fine distinctive Single Malt, excellent as a pre-dinner drink.

10
YEARS OLD

43%alc/vol   750ml

DISTILLED AT THE GLENKINCHIE DISTILLERY
PENCAITLAND SCOTLAND

SOLE DISTRIBUTOR IN USA, SCHIEFFELIN & SOMERSET CO, NEW YORK, N.Y. PRODUCT OF SCOTLAND

The entire production of Glenkinchie was used for blending until 1989, when a 10 year old version became available. This malt is a major component in the Haig family of blended whiskies, of which Haig and Haig Pinch is the most well known in the United States. Glenkinchie is a dry, light, floral whisky exemplifying Lowland style. The distillery has a very interesting museum and visitor center.

"Happy, smooth, appealing."

AROMAS: Spicy, a bit hot, clean.

FLAVORS: Medium weight, spicy, caramel, vanilla, dry mouth feel.

The Glenlivet

Highland (Speyside)

AGE WHEN BOTTLED: 12 year old, 18 year old, 21 year old; some independent bottlings, as well as special collectors' editions from the distillery.

STRENGTH: 12 year old, 40%; 18 year old and 21 year old, 43%.

Arguably the most famous single malt whisky in the world. Founded in 1824, The Glenlivet was the first licensed distillery in all of Scotland. Due to the efficiency of the operation and the high quality of the product, The Glenlivet was being exported by the mid-1860s. Because the whisky's reputation for quality was so great, many other distilleries in and around the Livet Glen adopted the name Glenlivet. In the 1880s, the owners of the distillery filed suit and were awarded the sole ownership of the name, The Glenlivet. A number of other distilleries in the region are allowed to use the name Glenlivet, but only as a hyphenated suffix, e.g. Longmorn-Glenlivet.

"Pretty to look at, very, very smooth—excellent all around."

AROMAS: 12 year old: oily, fruity, floral, slightly perfumed; 18 year old: peaty, a touch hot, nutty, honey, vanilla.

FLAVORS: 12 year old: sweet, fruity, a bit smoky, caramel finish; 18 year old: smoky, woody, coffee, tobacco, long, layered finish, a touch spicy.

Glenlossie

Highland (Speyside)

AGE WHEN BOTTLED: 10 year old.

STRENGTH: 40%.

Built in 1876, this distillery was taken over by Scottish Malt Distillers Ltd., in 1919. It is now owned by United Distillers. The majority of the production goes for blending, but there are single malts available.

"Nice for an after-dinner dram— quite light."

AROMAS: Perfumy and grassy.

FLAVORS: Nutty and smooth with a little fruit.

Glenmorangie

glen-mor-an-gy

Highland (Northern)

AGE WHEN BOTTLED: 10 year old, 12 year old, 18 year old.

STRENGTH: 10 year old, 40%; 18 year old, 43%; 12 year old, 56.5%.

Legend has it that on the site of Glenmorangie, one form of alcoholic beverage or another has been produced since the Middle Ages. This distillery was also known for making various technical advances through innovative still design. A series of 12 year old whiskies finished in different casks (sherry, port, and madeira) are available. Tasting those side by side was very interesting. Tasting notes refer to 18 year old.

"Class act. Muscular yet svelte."

AROMAS: Nutty, floral hints, oily-tasting.

FLAVORS: Smoky, coffee, tobacco, a touch of saltiness in the finish, full-flavored.

*G*lenturret

Highland (Southern)

AGE WHEN BOTTLED: 12 year old, 15 year old, 18 year old.

STRENGTH: 12 year old, 40%; 15 year old, 50%; 18 year old, 40%.

Competition continues between Glenturret and Edradour over the claim of smallest distillery in Scotland. Glenturret, established in 1775, was bought in 1959, and under the skilled guidance of James Fairlie, has produced numerous award-winning whiskies through the years. In 1981, Glenturret was bought by French liqueur makers, Cointreau SA; and then taken over in 1990 by Highland Distilleries, Co. Tasting notes refer to 12 year old.

"Very creamy." "Smooth finish."

AROMAS: Peaty, grassy, and full-bodied.

FLAVORS: Creamy and zesty.

Highland Park

Island (Orkney)

AGE WHEN BOTTLED: 12 year old; many independent bottlings.

STRENGTH: 12 year old, 40%; independent bottlings of various strengths.

Highland Park sits on what was originally the site of an illicit still run by Magnus Eunson. Mr. Eunson was also the local preacher, and managed to evade tax officials by hiding his whisky in a number of creative locations. According to some, this distillery was clandestinely operating since the 1790s, but then became licensed as a legitimate business in 1824. The peat used for malting the barley is locally grown and mixed with heather, which is said to add a distinctive note to the whisky. Tasting notes refer to 12 year old, 43% distillery bottle.

"I like this!!!"

AROMAS: Nutty, faintly oily, peaty.

FLAVORS: Smoky, caramel, fruity-peach and citrus, a hint of salt, long finish.

123

*I*mperial

Highland (Speyside)

AGE WHEN BOTTLED: Only independent bottlings available.

STRENGTH: Various.

Imperial was part of a group consisting of Dailuaine and Talisker. This distillery closed and reopened several times over the course of the last century. Its whisky has all been used for blending. An occasional independent bottling turns up from time to time.

"Very easy to drink, not too explosive."

AROMAS: Spicy, a little nutty.

FLAVORS: Slight touch of vanilla.

Inchgower

Highlands (Speyside)

AGE WHEN BOTTLED: 14 year old.

STRENGTH: 43%.

The Tochineal Distillery, built in 1824 and located at the mouth of the Spey River, was originally the site of what is now Inchgower. The distillery, however, was moved in 1936 to a spot near the coast, in search of larger quarters and a more reliable water source. Inchgower was acquired by Arthur Bell & Sons, which subsequently became a part of United Distillers.

"Perfect for an after-dinner dram."

AROMAS: Rich with vanilla.

FLAVORS: Buttery and sweet.

Knockando

Highland (Speyside)

AGE WHEN BOTTLED: 12 year old, 15 year old, 18 year old, 21 year old.

STRENGTH: 12 year old and 15 year old, 40%; 18 and 21 year old, 43%.

This distillery reopened in 1904 and was acquired in 1952 by the producers of J&B. Much of the whisky is used in blending, but the distillery has a fairly large capacity, so that it is easily found at retail. The whisky is bottled not according to a specific calendar, but when the distillery manager feels it is at its peak. The bottle bears both the date of distillation and the date of bottling. "Extra Old Reserve"—21 year old—is also available, although sometimes it turns out to be even a little older than 21 years. A whisky that lies about its age…

"Soft and easy."

AROMAS: Spicy, nutty, and a bit hot on the nose.

FLAVORS: Light, peppery, clean finish.

*L*agavulin

la-ga-voo-lin or lagga-voolin

Islay

AGE WHEN BOTTLED: 10 year old,
15 year old, 16 year old.

STRENGTH: 10 year old, 40%; 15 year old,
64.4%; 16 year old, 43%.

Claim is made that distilling has taken place
on this site as far back as 1742. The distillery
now known as Lagavulin was built during the
early part of the last century, probably in the
1820s. The majority of this whisky is used for
blending. In its early days, most of Lagavulin's
production was used as the base for White
Horse blended whisky. Tasting notes refer to
16 year old.

"Reminds me of the ocean."

AROMAS: Peat, iodine, floral.

FLAVORS: Smoky, very peaty, salty,
full-bodied.

BY APPOINTMENT TO
HER MAJESTY THE QUEEN
SCOTCH WHISKY DISTILLERS
HITE HORSE DISTILLERS LTD. GLASGOW

LAGAVULIN
DISTILLERY
ESTᴰ 1816 ISLA
REGIST·ERED
Machiedfay

ISLA

AVULIN

SLAY MALT WHISKY

16 YEARS

TCH WHISKY

over rocky falls, steeped in mountain air and
led and matured in oak casks exposed to the sea
and smoky character. Time, say the Islanders,
FIRE but LEAVES IN THE WARMTH

SUINABHAL" — By William Black — "I hef been in the
and I hef been . . . the . . . ulin Distillery and there

129

Laphroaig

la-froig

Highland (Northern)

AGE WHEN BOTTLED: 10 year old and 15 year old.

STRENGTH: 10 year old, 40%; 15 year old, 43%.

Built around 1820, this distillery produces a very individual whisky. Popular wisdom has it that close proximity to the coast contributes a distinctly briny or saline quality to the whisky. Many producers hold that the exchange of salt air and whisky in barrel creates this unique flavor. Laphroaig's producers believe that it is the high content of moss in the peat used during the malting process that gives the whisky its unique flavor. Another nice note that adds "flavor" to the character of this distillery is that in 1954 the owner left the distillery to Bessie Williamson, the company secretary. She ran the company quite successfully until she retired in 1972.

"A love-it or hate-it whisky."

AROMAS: 10 year old: peaty, smoky, medicinal; 15 year old: medicinal, peaty, citrus.

FLAVORS: 10 year old: iodine, smoky, quite intense saltiness, finishes sharply. 15 year old: a touch sweet, peppery, smoky, long sweet, sour finish.

Linkwood

Highland (Speyside)

AGE WHEN BOTTLED:
12 year old.

STRENGTH: 40%.

Built around 1821, Linkwood was expanded in the late 1860s. Rumor has it that one of the still masters was so convinced that any change in the still house would affect the whiskey's character that he refused to have even a spider's web removed.

"Light as a feather."

AROMAS: Sweet, faintly peaty aromas.

FLAVORS: Caramel, sweetish, very clean.

750ml

40%alc/vol
(80Proof)

PRODUCT OF   SCOTLAND

YEARS **15** OLD

Linkwood

SINGLE
HIGHLAND MALT

Scotch Whisky

•

PROPRIETORS
JOHN McEWAN & CO. LTD.

BONDED AND BOTTLED BY
GORDON & MACPHAIL · ELGIN

UNBLENDED   POT STILL

Littlemill

Lowland

AGE WHEN BOTTLED: 8 year old; some independent bottlings.

STRENGTH: 8 year old, 40% and 43%.

Possibly Scotland's oldest Lowland distillery—it appears that some form of brewing and then distilling has been performed on this site since the 14th century. Classified as a Lowland distillery, Littlemill uses water and peat from Highland sources. Most of the whisky produced is used in blending, but the distillery bottled some single malt, which is still available. Littlemill is now closed.

"First it explodes and then it smoothes out."
"It tastes like butterscotch."

AROMAS: Spicy, hot, a touch nutty.

FLAVORS: Sweet, vanilla, caramel, peachy, a bit peppery on the finish.

Loch Lomond-Inchmurrin

Highland (Southern)

AGE WHEN BOTTLED: 9 year old, 10 year old, 12 year old, 17 year old, 20 year old, 28 year old.

STRENGTH: 9 year old, 64%; 10 year old, 40%; all others, 43%.

Loch Lomond-Inchmurrin became operational in 1966. Built on the site of an old printing plant, the distillery sits right on top of the imaginary line that divides Highland from Lowland. The stills used at Loch Lomond are designed to distill different weights of whisky. In addition to producing Inchmurrin, the distillery also produces a stronger whisky called Rhosdhu.

"This stuff is very weird."

AROMAS: Rubbery, nutty, cheesy nose.

FLAVORS: Hot, a bit green, woody, strong, unbalanced character.

*L*ongmorn

Highland (Speyside)

AGE WHEN BOTTLED: 12 year old, 15 year old.

STRENGTH: 12 year old, 40%; 15 year old, 45%.

Longmorn distillery began operations in 1897, and along with Glen Grant was acquired by The Glenlivet distilleries in 1970. A corruption from the Gaelic, Longmorn means "the place of the holy man." The distillery was built on a site that was previously thought to house an ancient chapel. Tasting notes refer to the 15 year old.

"No one outstanding character, but pleasant to drink."

AROMAS: Caramel.

FLAVORS: Sweet.

DISTILLED AND BOTTLED IN SCOTLAND
PRODUCE OF SCOTLAND

LONGMORN

Highland Single Malt

SCOTCH WHISKY

This outstanding single malt whisky is produced only at the
Longmorn distillery, which stands on the site of an ancient abbey,
in the heart of the Scottish Highlands.

IMPORTED BY LONGMORN DISTILLING CO, NY, NY

MATURED IN OAK CASKS
**AGED
15
YEARS**

750 ML.

ALC. 45%
BY VOL.

The Macallan

Highland (Speyside)

AGE WHEN BOTTLED: 7 year old, 10 year old, 12 year old, 18 year old, and 25 year old.

STRENGTH: 7 year old and 10 year old, 40%; all others, 43%.

The Macallan was officially licensed to operate and pay taxes in 1824 (a few months after The Glenlivet became legal). It was founded on a site which was surely used for illicit distilling, in a great, secluded location with access to abundant sources of peat, barley and fresh water. The distillery was bought by Roderick Kemp, a larger-than-life figure in the history of the whisky business. His descendants are still involved in the operation of The Macallan. Some of the distinctive features of this distillery are its use of small, squat, copper pot-stills (whose shape is said to contribute to a creamy style of whisky) and its use of oak barrels seasoned with sherry to hold the whisky during maturation. The sherry-seasoned barrels set The Macallan apart; other distillers use bourbon-, port-, or Madeira-flavored barrels. Sherry barrels used to be quite common, because the sherry shipped from Spain to England came in its own barrels, which were expensive to send back empty to the sherry bodegas. The used barrels were therefore snapped up cheaply by whisky distilleries as the perfect aging vessels. Oak barrels seasoned with sherry, particularly dry oloroso, imparts lovely flavors and aromas into aging Scotch whisky. In recent times, sherry has been exported in stainless steel containers, so now this distillery has to commission sherry casks for the aging of its whisky.

In the spring of 1997, two monumental events occurred: a bottle of 1874 Macallan was discovered in the hold of a sunken ship and sold at auction (back to the distillery), and the distillery was purchased by Highland-Suntory. In the case of the former event, a replica of the 1874 was produced and sold (about that more, later). As regards the latter, Highland-Suntory has declared that it has no intention of changing anything about The Macallan except to increase production by six times. The Luddite in me rebels.

"Favorite." "My favorite." "Definitely the best." "My absolute favorite."

AROMAS: 12 year old: fruity, sherried, vanilla; 18 year old: caramel, toffee, hint of smoke, nutty. I had exactly one swallow of the commemorative 1874 at a press release: orange marmalade, vanilla, bitter chocolate.

FLAVORS: 12 year old: citrus, a touch salty, hint of smoke, long, slightly oily finish; 18 year old: very smooth, complex, vanilla, caramel, tobacco, nutty, long, very layered finish. Heavy, rich chocolate, orange, molasses, long, dark finish.

141

Mortlach

Highland (Speyside)

AGE WHEN BOTTLED: Various independent bottlings including: 12 year old, 15 year old, 21 year old, 22 year old.

STRENGTH: 12 year old, 15 year old and 21 year old, 40%; 22 year old, 46% and 65% (natural cask strength).

"Ay, I love the dram that comes from over the bowl-shaped valley." This remark was commonly made between friends in Dufftown, Scotland, around 1824. In Gaelic, Mortlach means bowl-shaped valley. The brand name now stands as a quaint reminder of the inextricable relationship between Scotch whisky and geography. Mortlach is used as major component in several blends, including Johnnie Walker Red Label. A large distillery, initially modernized in 1903, Mortlach has operated continuously since 1823 (except for a brief interruption during World War II). Tasting notes refer to 15 year old Gordon & MacPhail bottling.

"Well structured, the flavor unfurls."

AROMAS: Light, fresh, fruity.

FLAVORS: Smoky, woody, hints of vanilla, caramel. More layered than nose would indicate.

143

North Port

Highland (Eastern)

Age when bottled: 13 year old independent Glen Haven bottling.

Strength: 64%.

North Port was founded in the 1820s by a local farmer. It was named after the north gate in the walls that surrounded the city in ancient times. North Port closed in 1983 and has since been demolished.

"Very, very hot; not too groovy."

Aromas: Medicinal, smoke, citrus peel.

Flavors: Rubbery

Oban

Highland (Western)

Age when bottled: 12 year old, 14 year old.

Strength: 12 year old, 40%; 14 year old, 43%.

Claim has it that Oban has the record for continuous operation beginning in 1794. The duration and fortitude of Oban is reflected in its distinctive and complex single malts. The distillery was acquired by Scottish Malt Distillers Ltd., and closed briefly for one year in 1968. Tasting notes refer to 12 year old.

"This is a very savory, smoky single malt— it is delicious."

Aromas: Nutty, smoky, spicy.

Flavors: Smoky and smooth.

Old Fettercairn

Highland (Eastern)

AGE WHEN BOTTLED: 10 year old Distillers independent bottling.

STRENGTH: 43%.

Old Fettercairn has been producing whisky since (at least) 1824. According to one source, Sir John Gladstone (the father of William Gladstone, famous prime minister of Britain), was chairman of the board of this distillery. The younger Gladstone, who enacted numerous reforms throughout his political career, was instrumental in allowing bottled whisky to be sold to the general population. Almost all of Old Fettercairn is used in blending.

"Very long finish, quite balanced."

AROMAS: Melon, banana.

FLAVORS: Honeyed, banana, sweet.

Old Pulteney

Highland (Speyside)

AGE WHEN BOTTLED: 8 year old, 12 year old, 18 year old.

STRENGTH: 8 year old, 40%; 12 year old, 43%; 18 year old, 59.1%.

James Henderson founded Pulteney in 1826, and it subsequently closed from 1926 to 1951. Purchased in 1955 by Hiram Walker, Pulteney is used almost exclusively for blending; however, an 8 year old single malt is available and was used for our tasting.

"Light and fresh, well worth trying."

AROMAS: Slight spice and sweet nose.

FLAVORS: Peaty and slightly smoky.

Port Ellen

Islay

AGE WHEN BOTTLED: 14 year old.

STRENGTH: 43%.

Established in 1825, this distillery was silent from 1929 to 1966. Major renovations were made in 1967, instituting the use of four stills. The maltings continue to supply many Islay distilleries but Port Ellen stopped production in 1983.

"A rich and satisfying dram."

AROMAS: Peaty, smoky, and petroly.

FLAVORS: Oaky, buttery, and smoky.

Rosebank

Lowland

AGE WHEN BOTTLED: 12 year old, 17 year old.

STRENGTH: 12 year old, 43%; 17 year old, 43%.

James Rankine established Rosebank on the site of the prior Camelon distillery in 1840. It was rebuilt by his son in 1864. Rosebank's process involved triple distilling with one wash still and two spirit stills. The distillery enjoyed a fine reputation for many years and in 1914 the Rosebank Distillery was one of the founders of Scottish Malt Distillers—now part of United Distillers. Rosebank closed in May, 1993. Tasting notes refer to 12 year old.

"Nice balance of sweetness and spice."

AROMAS: Petrol and grass tones.

FLAVORS: Peaty and full-bodied.

Royal Brackla

Highland (Northern)

AGE WHEN BOTTLED: 10 year old.

STRENGTH: 43%.

Use of the prefix "Royal" was granted to this whisky in a show of approval by King William IV in 1835. In 1898 Brackla Distillery Company was formed, and more land was acquired for expansion from the Earl of Cawdor not far from Cawdor Castle. After a few changes of hands, the distillery was modernized in 1965. Steam-fired stills with a capacity of 5,000 gallons each were added.

"Smoky and pleasant, very enjoyable."

AROMAS: Clean, fruity, and peaty.

FLAVORS: A sweet, yet well-balanced fullness.

Royal Lochnagar

Highland (Eastern)

AGE WHEN BOTTLED: 12 year old and "selected reserve" (no age given).

STRENGTH: 12 year old, 40%; reserve, 43%.

Lochnagar became the distillery to the royal household at the time of Queen Victoria; hence the name "Royal." The phrase "take a peg of John Begg" was an early advertising slogan used by Royal Lochnager, as this distillery was built by John Begg in 1845. Much of this whisky is used in blending. Various individual casks of different ages are bottled occasionally and sold as Royal Lochnagar "Selected Reserve."

"Amazing length." "Excellent, bright, happy."

AROMAS: Floral, fruity, good aromatics.

FLAVORS: Pepper, hint of vanilla, woody, very persistent, lingering finish.

*S*capa

Island (Orkney)

AGE WHEN BOTTLED: No longer operating,
various independent bottlings: 8 year old,
10 year old, 14 year old.

STRENGTH: 40%.

Located on the very beautiful—if you like savage—
island of Orkney, this distillery opened in 1885 and
produced whisky until 1993. Tasting notes refer to a
10 year old, independent bottle.

*"I'd love to sip it at the beach on a cool July
evening."*

AROMAS: Oily nose, a bit of fruit and vanilla.

FLAVORS: Some caramel and vanilla, oily finish.

The Singleton
(of Auchroisk)

awk-ro-isk

Highland (Speyside)

AGE WHEN BOTTLED: 10 year old, 12 year old.

STRENGTH: 10 year old, 43%; 12 year old, 59.3%.

The owners, International Distillers and Vintners, built this 1974 Auchroisk distillery primarily as another source to add to its blended whiskies. The Singleton, however, is its single malt which has been widely praised. It retains its individuality from the main Auchroisk operation which can produce up to 1.5 million gallons per year.

"Delicious and satisfying. A real winner."

AROMAS: Fresh, fruity, and sweet; a little smoky.

FLAVORS: Creamy, coffee, and sweet.

Strathisla

strath-eye-la

Highland (Speyside)

AGE WHEN BOTTLED: 12 year old and many independent bottlings.

STRENGTH: 12 year old, 43%; independent bottlings in various strengths.

Strathisla started in 1786, and also claims to be the oldest distillery in Scotland. Once called Milton distillery, its name was changed to Strathisla in the 1950s. The spring from which the distillery draws its water is reputed to have supplied water to brewers and distillers in the region for over 600 years. Much of the whisky is used for blending, primarily in Chivas Regal.

"Very intense and layered."

AROMAS: Spicy, a little hot, lots of nut aromas.

FLAVORS: Smoky, woody, nutty, long weighty finish.

*T*alisker

Island (Skye)

AGE WHEN BOTTLED: 10 year old.

STRENGTH: 45.8%.

Talisker, the only distillery on the island of Skye, is a terrific example of the "seaweedy" character that island malts possess. One wonders if this flavor really exists or is a case of very pleasant poetic license.

"Tastes like hickory."
"Very classy stuff."
"Tastes like Band-Aids®." *(a very common comparison used for smokiness)*

AROMAS: Earthy, dark, smoky.

FLAVORS: Very peaty, woody, smoky, saline, long finish.

159

*T*amdhu

tam-doo

Highland
(Speyside)

AGE WHEN BOTTLED: 10 year old, no age given, various independent bottlings.

STRENGTH: No age given and 10 year old, 40%.

Very popular in England and Scotland, this whisky distiller does its own maltings. Tamdhu was closed from 1927 until 1947. It reopened and over the years has slowly expanded, and ultimately completely modernized in the 1980s.

"That is right up my alley, like apples and pears."
"Nice, long, balanced finish."

AROMAS: Fruity, floral.

FLAVORS: Sweet, smoky, honey, and spice.

Tamnavulin- Glenlivet

Highland (Speyside)

AGE WHEN BOTTLED: 10 year old, 18 year old.

STRENGTH: 10 year old, 40%; 18 year old, 46%.

Tamnavulin in Gaelic means "mill on the hill," which is an accurate description of this distillery that was built near an old mill, on the Glen, in the foothills of the Cairngorm Mountains in 1966. Tasting notes refer to 10 year old.

"A great all-around drinking malt."

AROMAS: Flowery nose, light.

FLAVORS: Peaty, oaky, and nutty.

Tobermory

Island (Mull)

AGE WHEN BOTTLED: None stated.

STRENGTH: 43.4%.

The only distillery on the island of Mull, this distillery has been closed and reopened a number of times since its founding. After being closed in 1989, the distillery was reopened in 1993. Older stocks of whisky can sometimes be found bottled under the label Ledaig (untasted).

"Pleasant with slightly explosive finish."

AROMAS: Grassy, minty.

FLAVORS: Spearmint.

Tomatin

Highland (Northern)

AGE WHEN BOTTLED: 10 year old.

STRENGTH: 43%.

Tomatin, one of Scotland's largest distilleries, was acquired by the Japanese in 1985. It was the first Scottish distillery to be purchased by the Japanese. Founded in 1897 by the Tomatin Spey District Distillery Co. Ltd., this house grew from four stills in 1956 to 23 stills in 1974. Most of the malt goes for blending and export, but it is also available as a single malt whisky.

"Very easy going down, with the slightest hint of sweetness."

AROMAS: Light and sweet.

FLAVORS: Smoky, medium-bodied, smooth.

Tomintoul-Glenlivet

Highland (Speyside)

AGE WHEN BOTTLED: 8 year old, 12 year old.

STRENGTH: 8 year old, 40%; 12 year old, 43%.

Two Glasgow whisky brokers established Tomintoul
in 1964 in the highest village in the Scottish
Highlands. It lies close to the Glenlivet area, hence its
name, and produces a total of one million gallons per
year. The founding brokers subsequently merged
with White & Mackay, Ltd., so much of this whisky
goes into White & Mackay blends. Tasting notes refer
to 12 year old.

"Extremely light and smooth."

AROMAS: Sweet, vanilla, and fruity.

FLAVORS: Smoky and clean; slightly spicy finish.

Tullibardine

Highland (Southern)

AGE WHEN BOTTLED: 10 year old.

STRENGTH: 40%.

In 1949 Tullibardine was built on the site of a seventeenth-century brewery. The distillery was bought by Invergordon Distillers, Ltd., in 1972. The whisky production greatly benefits from the excellent water it receives from the nearby Moor of Tullliburdine.

"Light and slightly smoky."

AROMAS: Full and fruity.

FLAVORS: Spicy, round; peppery finish.

*B*lended *Whiskies*

Before 1853, for Scotsmen who liked their brown spirits, single malt whisky was the only drink in town, so to speak. In that year, however, the whisky merchant Andrew Usher changed everything; he's the man who is credited with inventing blended whisky.

While malt whisky is produced from 100 percent, mostly malted barley, blended whisky contains between 20 and 50 percent malt whisky. The balance is made up of grain whisky. Grain whisky differs from malt whisky in that it is made from a number of different—less expensive—grains besides barley. Grain whisky, too, is produced in a continuous still, not a pot still. The upshot being that grain whisky, as compared to malt whisky, is pretty light and flavorless—not too good on its own, but just perfect for mixing with more strongly flavored whisky.

Once blended whisky was introduced, it became, for a variety of economic, social, and aesthetic reasons, synonymous with Scotch whisky. The ease of production of this new whisky, coupled with the lighter flavor profile and consistent quality, caught the consumer's fancy—and held it—until well into the 1980s. This was the first decade, at least as far as the United States was concerned, that blended whisky sales showed any sign of declining. That trend has continued, but curiously, over the past two decades, as sales of blended whisky and hard liquor in general have dropped, the single malt whisky market has grown exponentially.

Why should this be so? Tastes definitely change. Drinkers' palates become fatigued, we become jaded in our habits. Always on the look-out for new sensations, cutting edge consumers rediscovered the richer pleasures of single malts, the mania for consistency giving way to a spirit of adventure.

When a master blender goes about his work, adventure is definitely not on his agenda. His primary interest is to erase any and all characteristics that smack too much of regionalism, intensity, harshness, or any other quality that may be construed as too "individual." To this end, he will blend so much of this Highland whisky (for flavor) with that much Island whisky (for aroma) and that much Lowland whisky (for body). These blends may include as many as 50 single malts, which are combined in a large vat; during the writing of this book, a new "boutique" blend was introduced that combined 100 single malts. The master blenders all have their own recipes; one will add his predetermined percentage of grain whisky at this point, while another will add the grain whisky at a later stage, stir it thoroughly and put it into the cask. One will age his whisky for a few months, while another will leave it for three to four years to "marry" the flavors. These time-honored and top-secret recipes are adhered to scrupulously, producing year in and year out the consistent blends that the consumer can taste even before they are poured into the glass.

Lest you think I am bashing blended whisky, nothing could be further from the truth. I find, as you will see in the following tasting notes, that all of this research and experimentation in the name of consistency has produced some really very good blended whiskies. It's just that, having come this far in our search, having realized the joys that whisky can evoke in a receptive drinker, why settle for a pleasant dram when one can discover true greatness in the form of one's favorite single malt?

*B*lended Whisky Comparisons

Dewar's
"A very flavorful, enjoyable and easy drink."
AROMAS: Vaguely peppery, mild.
Flavors: Slightly sweet.

Chivas Regal
"Volatile—a lot of heat on the nose, really nice."
AROMAS: Wood-note, cedar.
Flavors: Coffee, toffee, rich and buttery.

Black Label
"I think it's good stuff."
"Very volatile."
AROMAS: Peppery, spicy.
Flavors: Petrol, pepper.

The Famous Grouse
"Very fresh on the nose."
"Soft mouth feel, very simple."
AROMAS: Slightly grassy and light.
Flavors: Well-balanced.

The Famous Grouse— Gold Reserve
"Explodes with a spicy punch."
AROMAS: Fresh, orange peel, spices.
Flavors: Orange, cinnamon, spice.

173

*B*lended Scotch Whisky

The following is a list of the most popular blended Scotch whisky brands now available with their age and proof.

Ballantine Scotch	17 year old	86 proof
Ballantine Scotch	30 year old	86 proof
Ballantine Scotch Finest		86 proof
Ballantine Scotch Gold Seal	12 year old	86 proof
Barrister Scotch		80 proof
Bellows Scotch		80 proof
Black & White Scotch		80 proof
Black Bull Scotch		100 proof
Buchanan's Scotch	12 year old	80 proof
Buchanan's Scotch Deluxe	18 year old	80 proof
Bullock & Lade (B&L) Scotch		80 proof
Chivas Regal Scotch	12 year old	80 proof
Clan MacGregor Scotch		80 proof
Claymore Scotch		80 proof
Cluny Scotch	12 year old	80 proof
Crawford's Scotch		80 proof
Crown Sterling Scotch		
Cutty Sark Scotch		80 proof
Desmond & Duff Scotch	12 year old	80 proof
Dewar's Scotch	12 year old	80 proof
Dewar's Scotch White Label		80 proof
Glenandrew Scotch	10 year old	
Glenandrew Scotch	15 year old	
Glenandrew Scotch	20 year old	
Grand Macnish Scotch		80 proof
Grand Old Parr Scotch Deluxe	12 year old	86 proof
Grant's Scotch Blended		80 proof
Grant's Scotch Decanter Toby Jug	25 year old	86 proof
Haig & Haig Scotch Dimple Pinch	15 year old	86 proof
Hankey Bannister Scotch		86 proof
Hartley Parker's Scotch		80 proof

174

Harvey's Scotch		80 proof
Heather Glen Scotch		80 proof
House of Stuart Scotch	4 year old	80 proof
Inver House Scotch Rare		80 proof
Inverarity Scotch Blended		
J & B Scotch Rare		80 proof
J & B Scotch Select		80 proof
J & B Scotch J.E.T.	15 year old	86 proof
J.W. Dant Scotch		80 proof
John Barr Scotch Gold Label		80 proof
John Barr Scotch Special Reserve Black Label		86 proof
John Begg Scotch Blue Cap		86 proof
John Player Scotch		80 proof
Johnnie Walker Scotch Black Label	12 year old	86.8 proof
Johnnie Walker Scotch Blue Label		80 proof
Johnnie Walker Scotch Red Label		80 proof
Johnnie Walker Scotch Gold Label	18 year old	
King George IV Scotch		80 proof
King William IV Scotch		80 proof
Legacy Scotch		80 proof
McColl's Scotch		80 proof
McGregor Scotch Perfection		80 proof
Old Smuggler Scotch		80 proof
Lauder's Scotch		80 proof
Passport Scotch		80 proof
Peter Dawson Scotch Special		80 proof
Piper 100 Scotch		80 proof
Poland Spring Scotch		80 proof
Queen Anne Scotch		80 proof
Royal Salute Scotch		80 proof
Royal Salute Scotch	21 year old	
Scoresby Scotch Very Rare		80 proof
Teacher's Scotch Highland Cream		86 proof
The Famous Grouse Scotch		80 proof
The Famous Grouse Scotch Gold Reserve		
Usher's Scotch Green Stripe		82 proof
White Horse Scotch		80 proof
Whiteside Scotch Blended		86.8 proof

Single Malt Scotch Menu

With the increasing popularity of single malts, many fine restaurants have added a separate Scotch listing to their wine and after-dinner drink lists. Keens Steakhouse, a venerable institution in New York City, has one of the best on-premise single malt lists that we have seen.

Keens STEAKHOUSE

SINGLE MALT SCOTCHES

SCOTCH	YEARS AGED	PRICE
HIGHLAND MALTS		
Ardbeg	20	12.00
Balblair	10	9.50
Clynelish	22	20.00
Dallas Dhu	1974	15.50
Dalmore	12	8.00
Dalmore Stillmans Dram	26	15.00
Dalwhinnie	15	9.50
Edradour	10	9.00
Glen Eden	NV	6.75
Glengoyne	10	9.00
Glengoyne	17	12.50
Glengoyne	1967	24.00
Glenkeith	1983	9.00
Glenlochy	25	23.00
Glenmorangie	10	7.50
Glenmorangie	18	10.50
Glenmorangie	12 *Port*	15.00
Glenmorangie	12 *Sherry*	10.00
Glenmorangie	12 *Madeira*	10.00
Glenmorangie	1971	26.50
Glenmorangie	1974	14.00
Glen Rothes	1979	11.00
Glen Rothes	10	7.50
Inchmurrin	10	8.00
Loch Dhu Black	14	9.00
Oban	10	6.75
Old Fettercairn	12	9.00
Royal Lochnagar	RESERVE	25.00
Royal Lochnagar	1971	13.00
Tomintoul	10	5.50
Tullibardine		
HIGHLAND/SPEYSIDE		
Aberfeldy	1978	11.00
Aberlour	10	8.00
Aberlour	1970	19.50
Balvenie	10	9.50
Balvenie	12	9.00
Balveni	15	10.00
Benriach	10	9.00
Benriach	1982	15.50
Cardhu	12	8.50
Cragganmore	12	9.00
Duftown	13	17.00
Glendronach	12	9.50
Glendronach	15	10.00
Glendeveron	12	6.75
Glenfarclas	10	7.00
Glenfarclas	12	7.50
Glenfarclas	25	15.50
Glenfiddich	12	7.00
Glenfiddich	18	18.00
Glenforres	12	5.50
Glenlivet	12	7.00
Glenlivet	18	11.00
Glentromie	12	8.00

SCOTCH   YEARS AGED   PRICE

HIGHLAND/SPEYSIDE—CONT.

SCOTCH	YEARS AGED	PRICE
LINKWOOD	21	
LONGMORN	1981	13.50
GLEN GARIOCH	8	10.50
GLEN GARIOCH	12	6.75
GLEN GARIOCH	15	7.00
GLEN GARIOCH	21	8.50
GLEN GLASSAUGH	12	13.00
GLEN MORAY	12	6.75
GLEN ORD	12	8.00
INCHGOWER	1980	9.00
KNOCKANDO	1980	10.50
KNOCKANDO	18	10.00
KNOCKANDO	25	12.50
KNOCKANDO	1970	25.00
MACALLAN	12	27.00
MACALLAN	18	9.00
MACALLAN	25	12.00
MORTLACH	22	25.00
STRATHISALA	12	19.50
TAMDHU	10	9.00
TORMORE	5	7.50
		6.25

LOWLAND

SCOTCH	YEARS AGED	PRICE
AUCHENTOSHAN	NV	
AUCHENTOSHAN	10	7.00
AUCHENTOSHAN	21	9.50
GLENKINCHE	10	16.50
INVERARITY	10	9.00
LITTLE MILL	8	9.00
PRIME MALT #1	15	7.50
ROSEBANK	1974	8.50
		11.50

ISLAY

SCOTCH	YEARS AGED	PRICE
BRUICHLADDICH	10	
BRUICHLADDICH	15	8.50
BRUICHLADDICH	21	10.50
BOWMORE LEGEND	NV	15.50
BOWMORE	10	7.50
BOWMORE	17	8.50
BOWMORE	21	10.50
BOWMORE	25	16.50
BOWMORE BLACK	1964	18.50
BUNNAHABHAIN	12	56.00
LAPHROAIG	10	9.50
LAPHROAIG	15	9.00
LAGAVULIN	16	13.00
PORT ELLEN	16	10.00
		11.50

CAMPLETOWN

SCOTCH	YEARS AGED	PRICE
DRAM SELECT	23	
DRAM SELECT	21	16.50
GLEN SCOTIA	12	14.50
SPRINGBANK	12	8.50
SPRINGBANK 100P	12	10.50
SPRINGBANK	15	11.00
SPRINGBANK	1979	12.50
SPRINGBANK	21	13.00
SPRINGBANK	25	15.00
		22.00

ISLE OF MULL

SCOTCH	YEARS AGED	PRICE
TOBERMORY	NV	
DRAM SELECT	21	7.00
		14.50

OLD MELDRUM

SCOTCH	YEARS AGED	PRICE
MICHEL COUVIER	15	
		10.50

ISLAND MALTS

SCOTCH	YEARS AGED	PRICE
HIGHLAND PARK	12	
SCAPA	1979	8.50
SCAPA	12	10.50
TALISKER	10	9.00
		9.50

IRISH SINGLE MALT

SCOTCH	YEARS AGED	PRICE
BUSHMILLS	10	
BUSHMILLS	16	8.00
* MIDLETON VERY RARE	BLEND	11.50
		16.50

ALL SCOTCHES SUBJECT TO AVAILABILITY

Glossary

Blended whisky • A combination of grain and malt whiskies, popular for their lighter styles of flavor.

Cask • A wooden barrel used to age Scotch whisky.

Continuous still • A coffey still, as opposed to a pot still, consists of two columns that do not need to be refilled, but can be used continuously. This process is used for making a lighter Scotch whisky typically used for blends.

Diastase • An enzyme contained within grain that allows starch to become soluble. The next step in distillation is to turn that starch into sugar.

Draff • The remaining grain, generally barley, left in the mash tun after the wort is drawn off. This material is dried and used as cattle feed.

Feints • The distillate that remains after the middle cut, or best bottling whisky, has been drawn off. Feints contain high levels of alcohol and impurities and are typically blended with the foreshots and the wash and redistilled.

Finishing • A form of aging. Certain whisky will be put into to various types of casks to marry and age.

Foreshots • The first part of the distillate to come out of the second kettle of the pot still. The foreshots have low alcohol levels and impurities and are therefore not bottled. They are saved and redistilled with the feints.

Grain whisky • Whisky made in a patent still. The primary grain is usually corn.

Independent bottler • A broker or firm which will seek out or contract with malt distilleries to purchase individual casks of malt whisky. The independent bottler uses its own private label usually indicating the origin of the distillery on it. Examples of classic independent bottlers are Cadenheads, Gordons & McPhail, and The Scotch Msalt Whisky Society.

Low wines • The distillate produced in the first kettle of the pot still. It contains alcohol, other chemical compounds of both pure and impure natures, and a bit of water. The low wines are redistilled in the spirit still.

Malt • Any grain whose starch has been converted into sugar; the primary sugar is maltose.

Mashing • Mixing dried ground malt with hot water.

Middle cut • The best of the distillate from the spirit still, as determined by the still operator. This is the only portion of the distillate that is bottled.

Patent still • Also called the continuous still, it can operate without interruption, unlike the pot still which needs to be cleaned and recharged after each pass. The production from the continuous still is a clean, light, rather characterless spirit, generally used for the production of grain alcohol.

Peat • There are two kinds of peat, marsh and forest. Marsh peat is made up of decomposed mosses. Forest peat is made up of decomposed branches and leaves. When used as a fuel source for drying malted barley, the peat imparts a distinctive flavor to malt whisky.

Pot still • A pair of copper kettles with coils at the top, heated by coal or steam. In the first of the two, called the wash still, the fermented liquid is heated to the boiling point and vaporizes into the coils. The coils are cooled and the vapor is condensed and collected. The production from the first still, known as the low wines, is put through the second vessel, called the spirit still, and malt whisky emerges.

Proof • The alcoholic strength of the spirit, measured with a hydrometer.

Rectify • To dilute with a percentage of water to achieve a uniform proof.

Saccharify • The production of sugar during the malting and soaking process. The enzyme diastase is released inside the barley during this process. The starch inside the grain is turned into sugar, hence, to saccharify.

Single malt whisky • The production of an individual distillery.

Spirit still • The second of the two pot stills producing the high concentration finished alcohol spirit which will be directly placed in casks. *(See Wash still)*

Uisge Beatha • Gaelic for "water of life." Over the centuries, this term was shortened, anglicized, and ultimately rendered as whisky.

Wash • The fermented wort. This liquid is placed in the pot still for the first distillation.

Wash still • The first of the two pot stills typical to Scotch whisky that will produce low concentration low wines.

Wort • The liquid that is produced by soaking malted barley in warm water in a large tub called a mash tun. This liquid contains sugars and other components that, with the addition of brewer's yeast, transform it into alcohol.

Distiller/ Producer Resource Guide

Aberlour
ABERLOUR, Banffshire
AB38 9PJ
Tel: 01340-871204/285
Fax: 01340-871729

Ardbeg
PORT ELLEN, Islay, Argyll
PA42 7DU
Tel: 01496-302244

Ardmore
KENNETHMONT,
Aberdeenshire AB54 4NH
Tel: 01464-831213
Fax: 01464-831428

Auchentoshan
DALMUIR, Dunbartonshire
G81 4SG
Tel: 01389-878561
Fax: 01389-877368

Aultmore
KEITH, Banffshire
AB55 3QY
Tel: 01542-882762
Fax: 01542-886467

Balbair
Edderton, TAIN, Ross-shire
IV19 1LB
Tel: 01862-821273
Fax: 01862-821360

The Balvenie
Dufftown, KEITH,
Banffshire AB55 4DH
Tel: 01340-820373
Fax: 01340-820805

Ben Nevis
FORT WILLIAM, Inverness-
shire PH33 6TJ
Tel: 01397-702476
Fax: 01397-702768

Benriach
Longmorn, ELGIN,
Morayshire IV30 3SJ
Tel: 01542-783400
Fax: 01542-783404

Bladnoch
BLADNOCH, Wigtownshire
DG8 9AB
Tel: 01988-402235

Bowmore
BOWMORE, Islay, Argyll
PA43 7JS
Tel: 01496-810441
Fax: 01496-810757

Bruichladdich
BRUICHLADDICH, Islay,
Argyll PA49
Tel: 01496-850221

Bunnahabhain
PORT ASKAIG, Islay, Argyll
PA46 7RP
Tel: 01496-840646
Fax: 01496-840248

Caol Ila
Port ASKAIG, Islay, Argyll
PA49 7UN
Tel: 01496-840207
Fax: 01496-840660

Caperdonich
ROTHES, Morayshire
AB38 7BS
Tel: 01542-783300

Cardhu
Knockando, ABERLOUR,
Banffshire AB38 7RY
Tel: 01340-810204
Fax: 01340-810491

Clynelish
BRORA, Sutherland
KW9 6LR
Tel: 01408-621444
Fax: 01408-621131

Cragganmore
BALLINDALLOCH,
Banffshire, AB37 9AB
Tel: 01807-500202
Fax: 01807-500288

Dallas Dhu
FORRES, Morayshire
IV36 0RR

The Dalmore
ALNESS, Ross-shire IV 0UT
Tel: 01349-882362
Fax: 01349-883655

Dalwhinnie
DALWHINNIE, Inverness-
shire PH19 1AB
Tel: 01528-22240
Fax: 01528-522240

Deanston
DOUNE, Pethshire
FK16 6AG
Tel: 01786-841422
Fax: 01786-841439

Dufftown-Glenlivet
Dufftown, KEITH,
Banffshire AB55 4BR
Tel: 01340-820224
Fax: 01340-820060

The Edradour
PITLOCHRY, Perthshire
PH16 5JP
Tel: 01796-473524
Fax: 01796-472002

Glen Garioch
Oldmeldrum, INVERURIE,
Aberdeenshire AB51 0ES
Tel: 01651-872706
Fax: 01651-872578

Glen Grant
ROTHES, Morayshire
AB38 7BS
Tel: 01542-783300
Fax: 01542-783306

Glen Keith
KEITH, Banffshire
AB55 3BU
Tel: 01542-783044
Fax: 01542-783056

Glen Ord
MUIR OF ORD, Ross-shire
IV6 7UJ
Tel: 01463-870421
Fax: 01463-870101

Glen Scotia
12 High Street, CAMPBEL-
TOWN, Argyll PA28 6DS
Tel: 01586-552288

The Glendronach
Forgue, HUNTLY,
Aberdeenshire AB54 6DB
Tel: 01466-730202
Fax: 01466-730202

Glenfarclas
Marypark, BALLINDAL-
LOCH, Banffshire
AB37 9BD
Tel: 01807-500209
Fax: 01807-500234

Glengoyne
DUMGOYNE, Stirlingshire
G63 9LB
Tel: 01360-550229
Fax: 01360-550094

Glenkinchie
PENTCAITLAND, East
Lothian EH34 5ET
Tel: 01875-340333
Fax: 01875-340854

Glenfiddich
Dufftown, KEITH,
Banffshire AB55 4DH
Tel: 01340-820373
Fax: 01340-820805

The Glenlivet
BALLINDALLOCH,
Banffshire AB37 9DB
Tel: 01542-783220
Fax: 01542-783220

Glenlossie
ELGIN, Morayshire
IV30 3SS
Tel: 01343-860331
Fax: 01343-860302

Glenmorangie
TAIN, Ross-shire IV19 1PZ
Tel: 01862-892043
Fax: 01862-893862

The Glenturret
The Hosh, CRIEFF,
Perthshire PH7 4HA
Tel: 01764-656565
Fax: 01764-654366

Highland Park
KIRKWALL, Orkney
KW15 1SU
Tel: 01856-873107
Fax: 01856-876091

Imperial
Carron, ABERLOUR,
Morayshire, AB38 7QP
Tel: 01340-810276
Fax: 01340-810563

Inchgower
BUCKIE, Banffshire
AB56 2AB
Tel: 01542-831161
Fax: 01542-834531

Knockando
Knockando, ABERLOUR,
Morayshire AB38 7RD
Tel: 01340-810205
Fax: 01340-810369

Lagavulin
PORT ELLEN, Islay, Argyll
PA42 7DZ
Tel: 01496-302400
Fax: 01496-302321

Laphroaig
PORT ELLEN, Islay, Argyll
PA42 7DU
Tel: 01496-302418
Fax: 01496-302496

Linkwood
ELGIN, Morayshire
IV30 3RD
Tel: 01343-547004
Fax: 01343-549449

Littlemill
BOWLING, Dunbartonshire
G60 5BG
Tel: 01389-874154

Loch Lomond-Inchmurrin
ALEXANDRIA,
Dunbartonshire G83 0TL
Tel: 01389-752781
Fax: 01389-757977

Longmorn
ELGIN, Morayshire
IV30 3SJ
Tel: 01542-783400
Fax: 01542-783404

Longrow
CAMPBELTOWN, Argyll
PA28 6ET
Tel: 01586-552085
Fax: 01586-553215

The Macallan
Craigellachie, ABERLOUR,
Banffshire AB38 9RX
Tel: 01340-871471
Fax: 01340-871212

Mortlach
Dufftown, KEITH,
Banffshire AB55 4AQ
Tel: 01340-820318
Fax: 01340-820018

Oban
Stafford Street, OBAN,
Argyll PA34 5NH
Tel: 01631-562110
Fax: 01631-563344

Old Fettercairn
Distillery Road,
LAURENCEKIEK,
Kincardineshire AB30 1YE
Tel: 0161-340244
Fax: 01561-340447

Old Pulteney
Huddart Street, WICK,
Caithness KW1 5BA
Tel: 019555-602371
Fax: 01955-602279

Port Ellen
PORT ELLEN, Islay, Argyll
PA42 7AJ

Rosebank
Camelon, FALKIRK,
Stirlingshire FK1 5BW
Tel: 01324-623325

Royal Brackla
Cawdor, NAIRN,
Nairnshire IV12 5QY ›
Tel: 01667-404280
Fax: 01667-404743

Royal Lochnagar
Crathie, BALLATER,
Aberdeenshire AB35 5TB
Tel: 01339-742273
Fax: 01339-742312

Scapa
KIRKWALL, Orkney
KW15 1SE
Tel: 01856-872071
Fax: 01856-876585

**The Singleton of
Auchroisk**
MULBEN, Banffshire
AB55 3XS
Tel: 01542-860333
Fax: 01542-860265

Strathisla
KEITH, Banffshire AB55 3BS
Tel: 01542-783049
Fax: 01542-783055

Talisker
CARBOST, Skye IV47 8SR
Tel: 01478-640203
Fax: 01478-640401

Tamdhu
Knockando, ABERLOUR,
Morayshire AB38 7RP
Tel: 01340-810221
Fax: 01340-810255

Tamnavulin-Glenlivet
BALLINDALLOCH,
Banffshire AB37 9JA
Tel: 01807-590285

Tobermory
TOBERMORY, Mull, Argyll
PA75 6NR
Tel: 01688-302645
Fax: 01688-302643

Tomatin
TOMATIN, Inverness-shire
IV13 7YT
Tel: 01808-511444
Fax: 01808-511373

Tomintoul-Glenlivet
BALLINDALLOCH,
Banffshire, AB37 9AQ
Tel: 01807-590274
Fax: 01807-590342

Tullibardine
Blackford, AUCHTER-
ARDER, Perthshire
PH4 1QG
Tel: 01764-682252